COTSW
FOLLIES AND ~~~CIES

A Guide to the Curious,
Whimsical and Romantic

MARGARET CAINE and ALAN GORTON

S.B. Publications

By the same authors:
Curiosities of Gloucestershire - The Cotswolds
Curiosities of Gloucestershire - The Severn Vale and Forest of Dean

**To two daughters,
for unfailing enthusiasm
and assistance**

First published in 1998 by S.B. Publications
c/o 19 Grove Road, Seaford, East Sussex BN25 1TP

ISBN 1 85770 163 1

Printed and bound by Island Press
Unit 3, Cradle Hill Industrial Estate, Seaford, East Sussex BN25 3JE.
Telephone: (01323) 490222

CONTENTS

Front cover: The Red House, Painswick.
Back cover: Lord Berner's Folly, Faringdon.
Title page: Finials, Banqueting House, Chipping Campden.

INTRODUCTION

What is it? Who built it? When and why? How often do we ask ourselves these questions when we see a strange building or an unusual garden? Do we even know where these are, for they are often hidden away from everyday view? The creative use of the imagination by many people living on the Cotswolds are the subject of this book: follies and eyecatchers, gazebos and belvederes, temples and pagodas, dairies and bath-houses, sham castles and artificial ruins. Like the demonic sprites of old, their buildings have adopted an endless series of disguises: not surprisingly, they have lent themselves to the English gift for eccentricity.

Of the 1,300 follies documented in the UK, the Cotswolds have a relatively high proportion. Survival has been capricious but many superb examples remain; not only isolated fantasies with the melancholy charm of neglect, but fine groups well preserved. All that is lost forever is a hermitage that still has its live hermit, a man paid to sit in a remote cave, hair and nails uncut, pondering on a skull.

Earlier than follies, buildings had been erected which were not subject to constraints of money - or planning consent. Outside the garden proper, in the parks and hunting-grounds that surrounded their great houses, the estate owners of the late Tudor, Jacobean and Stuart times erected 'stands', where spectators could watch the progress of the hunt, and at the same time enjoy the distant prospect of the countryside. Often these offered a series of rooms for entertainment, as they involved a long expedition from the main house. Gate houses to the park also had a number of functions, not only in announcing a visitor's arrival or in keeping unwanted visitors out: they provided splendid dining-rooms for shooting-party lunches or other forms of pleasure.

However, in the eighteenth century the British Isles were captivated by a craze for follybuilding, and no gentleman's estate was complete without one. Some aspired to a complete set: indeed, to have no eccentricities in the park was itself an eccentricity.

What is a folly? 'An eccentricity in stone', 'a structure built for pleasure before purpose', 'a practical joke in stone', 'Bedlam in architecture', phrases which describe structures erected without regard to the usual building practices and tastes, for purposes so bizarre or whimsical as to make their cost out of all proportion to any spurious utility. The point of a folly is that it has no point. It is the expression of a whim, constructed for mischief, obsession or pure joy.

As a generic term word, *folly* is often used to imply one of many types of decorative structures such as sham castles, sham bridges, pagodas, temples, pyramids, and so on but which are useless or inconsequential. Follies serve no purpose? How preposterous. They all amuse the guests and they certainly impress the neighbours; they ornament a gentleman's garden, and, importantly for us, provide a mirror to his mind. Some curious structures have an overtly practical purpose: pyramids and towers planted as memorials in the heart of the countryside, or eyecatchers intended to make a bold silhouette at a distance animate the horizon. Others serve nostalgia for the romantic but misconceived notion of the Middle Ages or for ancient Greece or Rome, or as pieces for entertainment, in the days when visitors followed the convention of going on long circular walks, with *'incidents'* revealing themselves at different angles, in different combinations. They were created to evoke mood, association and magic - the essence of follies.

The history of follies is one of diffusion from a few standard-bearers. Castles were the first to appear in the parks, but others followed quickly, and an eager improver could add other delights; or have them all; or invent something for himself. Any one of these might be designed in the Gothick, Roman, Chinese, Moorish, Greek or Druidical styles - they came into fashion roughly in that order, and could happily be used all at once. What was chosen for what site in what style depended on personal taste, place, money, materials and fashion; success was as capricious as survival has been.

Better called artificial ruins, sham ruins appeared, to give a medieval chivalric overtone or Gothic accent to an improved landscape and to direct the eye to a scenically desirable point and hold it there. They are not though to be despised as 'sham', for they themselves have now joined the realms of genuine antiquity. These ornamental or suggestive ruins had overtones of chivalry (the ruined castle) or of religion (the ruined church or abbey) and were regarded as historically appropriate to their English environment. Moreover, the ruin induced moral reflection on the transience of earthly things. In building such an imitation, vagueness of effect was held to be wrong: the imagination had to be engaged at once by knowing what the ruin represented:

> *"The mind must not be allowed to hesitate; it must be hurried away from examining into reality, by the exactness and the force of the resemblance".*

Ivy and shrubs helped with such picturesque ruins:

> *"An intermixture of a vigorous vegetation, intimates a settled despair of their restoration".*
> (Both quotations from Whatley's *Observations on Modern Gardening*, 1770)

and serves as a reminder of man's mortality and the transience even of his most noble creations.

Folly gardens had a spate, and in particular the development of grottos. To the ancient Greeks these were shady caves where offerings were made to the nymphs. To the Romans - and the equally imperious eighteenth-century English aristocracy - they were places of amusement, somewhere to sit on a hot day. Unlike follies, they are easy to define - a pleasant cave that may be natural, or 'nature-improved', or entirely artificial, made of rocks and sometimes decorated with shells and mirrors or broken ceramics - and often a Neptune in occupation. Water is also a traditional ingredient of a grotto: to drip from stalactites, gush in cascades, or sometimes just to sit serene and still.

Temples too came to litter large estates. These are generally in Classical style and follies in Gothick, but this is only part of the picture. There is also a difference in mood: a temple is a soothing ornament, a folly is an emotional response.

After about 1840, few romantic buildings were created: the fashion was over.

One man's folly ...

BROADWAY

Location Off the A44, one mile south-east of Broadway. Sheet 150   11263617

Prospect towers are relics of that movement in the eighteenth and nineteenth centuries which flowered in an appreciation of nature and scenery, was manifest in the paintings of the English landscape school and in the poems of Wordsworth, and led ultimately to our own sense of refreshment in the countryside. They are found in many shapes, round, square or octagonal, and were set up where they *'commanded the prospect'* or distant view.

> *Heav'ns, what a goodly prospect spreads around,*
> *Of hills, and dales, and woods, and lawns, and spires!*
> *And glittering towns, and gilded streams, till all*
> *The stretching landskip into smoke decays.*
>   James Thomson *The Seasons*

What an inspiration were these lines to the tower-builders, whose structures raised the hill-top, extended the *'prospect'* (preferably, as the concern for pure nature increased, a *'prospect'* uninterrupted by Thomson's *'glittering towns'*) and recalled more virtuous days by their medieval appearance. Builders were also inspired by the 'lantskip' passage in Milton's *L'Allegro*, on the pleasures of the eye:

> *Towers and Battlements it sees*
> *Boosom'd high in tufted Trees.*

Even then on one of the upper floors it was common to have a well-appointed room where ladies and gentlemen of the great house could dine or take tea, read the poets and meditate on the landscape, which looked still more ravishing from the castellated top. Even so, the towers were designed not only to be looked from, but also to be looked at. They were embellishments of the landscape.

> *The prospect-tower is a noble object to look at, and a gratifying and instructive position to look from. It should be placed on the highest grounds of a residence, in order to command as wide a prospect as possible, to serve as a fixed recognised point to strangers, in making a tour of the grounds.*

So wrote Loudon in his *Encyclopaedia of Gardening* of 1828, describing the rooms of a tower as *'resting-places'* - *'absolutely necessary, where ease and enjoyment are studied, and where some attention is had to the delicacy of women, and the frailties of old age'*.

Eventually, though, such towers came to be regarded as a joke to the new middle-class Victorians, who lumped them with sham ruins, landscape temples and so on as 'follies' - though 'folly' was used of such towers before the eighteenth century was out.

At Broadway, the 'broad way' is the main street, wide enough to take huge flocks of sheep and droves of cattle which passed through on their way to the London markets. The village remains anomalously in Worcestershire because the Estate was held by Pershore Abbey prior to the dissolution in 1539. It is though to the skyline in Gloucestershire that one's eye is drawn, to the hill which at 1,024 feet above sea level is the second highest point in the Cotswolds and named variously over the centuries Barrow Hill and "the Beacon", for it was a likely site for signal bonfires which transmitted news quickly from one end of the country to the other, such as the sighting of the Spanish Armada. Like a punctuation mark on this north-westerly tip of the Cotswolds and almost straddling the county boundary stands a dark, Norman-style, battlemented tower. The imposing structure was erected at the very end of the eighteenth century by George William, 6th Earl of Coventry, who commissioned James Wyatt to design a 'prospect', an improvement of the view from the Earl's Worcestershire estates, and is near his connecting Springhill estate bought by an earlier Lord Coventry in 1628.

The various reasons now given for the Tower being built are a mixture of sense, showmanship and whim. One is that it was built as a hunting lodge. Another, that it was a means of signalling to his home at Croome that the Earl was on his way there and for the servants to begin their preparations. Yet another, that the Tower was built not so much as a folly but as a present to satisfy the caprice of a wife.

The two devastatingly beautiful Gunning sisters took London by storm in the 1750s: unsophisticated daughters of an impoverished Irishman, they became the toast of the town. In 1752, Maria, the lovelier and though the eldest still only nineteen years of age, married the Earl of Coventry. Within eight years she had died a premature and terrible death from consumption, though a major contributory cause was the penetration through and blockage of her pores by lead in the pigment she used unsparingly as facial cosmetic.

Lord Coventry married again. This second Countess was a woman of great common sense who, when a tower was first proposed as an improvement to the view from Croome fifteen miles away as the crow flies, ordered a beacon to be lit on the top of Broadway Hill to make sure that it would indeed be plainly visible. When this had been done to her satisfaction, she called on all the local gentry to ensure the beacon could be seen from their estates also! She then persuaded the Earl to humour her as his new wife by having the Tower built in that exact spot.

The real reason, though, for both the construction and the location may be more prosaic, as the Coventrys were already familiar with follies at the family seat at Croome Court, including a Panorama Tower designed by Robert Adam in 1766. Moreover, Bredon Hill, on which there was already Parson's Folly, completely obscures Croome Court from Broadway Hill, so the only visual connection with their land was with Springhill, the estate they already owned.

In 1797, fireworks and a bonfire on the hill celebrated the one hundred years since the creation of the Earldom. Is it possible that that the Tower was planned as a memorial for this? Simultaneously though, it asserted the Earl's importance in Broadway which it overlooks from on high.

Whatever the actual reason for its being built, the Tower breaks several pleasant folly traditions. One was that at least 100 feet of solid hilltop should intercept the line of vision between any tower and either its object or its builder - but not in this case. Another, was that on a clear day an excessive number of counties can be seen from the top - thirteen in all instead of the more usual modest seven.

Just as with the reasons for building it, various dates are given for its construction: 1797, 1798, and 1800. The only thing we know for certain is that the plans were drawn up by the architect James Wyatt and are dated 1794.

This landmark is a castellated and machicolated hexagon with three round towers with canted sides at alternate angles, looking like a miniature Norman keep or, as it is set in the middle of a field, like a castle from some gigantic chess set. Wyatt followed the fashion set by Launcelot 'Capability' Brown for follies to be part of the estate landscaping but the design is rather ugly and the stonework, from further east and hence a darker colour than the native golden Guiting stone, chosen specifically to suggest a stark, brooding presence, is efficient consistent with the Countess and the visible county-list. The sixty-five foot Tower commands a panoramic view, which from the foot is only marginally less than from the battlemented top, embracing the fertile Evesham plain and the river Avon, the Malverns, the Clee and Clent Hills, and the distant heights of the Wrekin and the Black Mountains.

Put to use initially as a hunting box, after renovation work in 1827 the Tower became a dwelling house for various people. At one time it housed some of the collection, the largest ever amassed, of the bibliomaniac Sir Thomas Phillipps, including his private printing press. Later William Morris and fellow Pre-Raphaelites, the artist Edward Burne-Jones and the poet Dante Gabriel Rossetti, rented it for extended holidays. It was from here in 1876, following a visit to St. John's church at Burford and there witnessing the 'restoration' being carried out, that Morris wrote the letter which was to lead to the foundation of the Society for the Protection of Ancient Buildings and Monuments, or the 'Anti-Scrape Society' as it became known. Later the Tower served a more utilitarian purpose: during the Second World War the top floor made a magnificent observation post and headquarters for the Royal Observer Corps.

BREDON HILL

Bredon Hill is an outlier of the Cotswolds, eroded from the main bulk millennia ago. Rising from the level Vale of Evesham as an island in a sea of green, when shrouded in cloud a local weather rhyme warns

> *When Bredon Hill puts on his hat*
> *Ye men of the Vale, beware of that.*

It carries two follies. To reach the first requires a steep climb initially but is worth the expenditure of effort if only for the panoramic views across the plain where Shakespeare's Avon meanders lazily to the Severn, to

> *see the coloured counties and hear the larks so high,*

to quote from A E Housman's *A Shropshire Lad.*

An eighteenth-century squire of Kemerton and owner of Woollas Hall, Mr Parsons clearly felt the need to impose himself on nature by rounding off the height of the hill to a convenient figure of 1,000 feet above sea level, but with no reverence for the people who had lived there centuries before. Named Parson's Folly, this little square prospect tower with a viewing platform is constructed inside a 2,000-year-old hill fort. Sadly, it is now used to position communication aerials and dishes of many different sorts and sizes.

Bredon Hill being the same height as Broadway Hill and much nearer to Croome Court, the Earl of Coventry's palatial seat, the existence of Parson's Folly lends a touch of authenticity to the story of the Countess's dash round her neighbours, for it is just as suitable a site for a folly tower. Did Parsons beat the Coventrys to it, for his little tower dates from the late eighteenth century, before Broadway Tower? While ostensibly this prospect tower was constructed to complete the height of Bredon Hill at 1,000 feet, it could well have influenced the building of Broadway Tower which outshines it in every other respect.

Halfway up Bredon Hill (Sheet 150 85324061), the other folly is Bell's Castle, also known locally as 'the summer house'. Complete with battlements and lancet windows, all slightly different, it was built onto existing cottages in 1820 by Captain Edmund Bell, a smuggler. Unfortunately, building proved to be an expensive undertaking and he was forced to return to his trade at sea. Before long his nefarious deeds caught up with him. He was betrayed by a colleague over jealousy for the favours of a French woman, imprisoned and then hanged at Stratford in 1841; with some sardonic sense of humour the cause of his death was certified as "dropsy". Bell is believed to have been the last smuggler hanged in England. An illegitimate daughter from Cheltenham took his body and made arrangements for him to be buried at Pershore Abbey - certainly a conventional end to a colourful life.

WINCHCOMBE

Location Six miles north-east of Cheltenham, on the B4632. Sheet 163 02312833

Derived from the formal grottos of the Renaissance gardens of Italy, grottos of eighteenth and nineteenth century England were essential elements of the landscape garden. Gradually, they lost their more formal plan, their rococo decoration of shells, spars, minerals, etc., and their classical association with nymphs, and approximated to the natural cave, becoming improved versions of the water-caves of the English limestone districts. They are, though, less a feature of the countryside than an occasional tumbling relic of great gardens dismantled or in decay. Here though is a superb example, reflecting the remarkable history of this little town situated in a winding combe along a slope at the base of Langley Hill, and once the 'capital' of the long-forgotten Wincelcumshire, the second most important town in Saxon Gloucestershire and royal centre of the Hwicce sub-kingdom of Mercia.

The garden of Bleby House, in Abbey Terrace, slopes down to the river Isbourne and contains a small early-eighteenth-century grotto, roofed with curved stone slates and vaulted with stalactites decorated with shells. Here is one of the few grottos which may have been inspired by religious rather than fashionable sentiments, since Winchcombe was the site of the shrine of St. Kenelm, Cotswolds' own saint. The grotto is said to have been built on the spot where he died - though according to legend he was murdered at the instigation of his sister on the Clent Hills, several miles away.

St. Kenelm's Grotto

6

The story starts when Kenwulf (or Coenwulf or Kenulf) was the King of Mercia. He died in 819 AD and, according to legend, left as his heir and successor his seven-year-old son, Kenelm. Unfortunately, one of his two older sisters, Quendryda (or Cynefrith) wanted the kingdom for herself: on her father's death she set out to get it by fair means or foul. Her first attempt, to poison her little brother, failed. Next she bribed Kenelm's tutor, Askobert, to murder him. This dreadful task was accomplished while the pair were out hunting in Clent forest and, according to old manuscripts, the spirit of the child assumed the guise of a white dove and flew up to heaven. The Pope was celebrating Mass in Rome when to his astonishment he saw a dove hovering above him, carrying a scroll. The bird flew down and carefully placed it on the altar before him. It read:

In Clent cow pasture, under a thorn,
Of head bereft lies Kenelm, King born.

The Pope and all those with him gave thanks for the curious miracle, and the day, July 17, was set apart as St. Kenelm's Day. Papal ambassadors were sent to the Archbishop of Canterbury, who in turn passed an order to the Abbots of Winchcombe and Worcester, that the body of Kenelm should be recovered. The boy's body was found, and as soon as it was lifted reverently from its shallow grave a clear spring bubbled from the spot, which came to be regarded as a holy fountain.

When this news reached Quendryda, terrified she began to read the 108th Psalm backwards to put a curse on the monks who were bearing her small brother's body back to their Abbey. But as soon as she read aloud the verse *'Let this be the rewards of my adversaries'*, there occurred a horrible event: both her eyes popped out, covering the psalter with blood, and the wicked and evil Queen Quendryda died. No church would have her body for burial, and it was flung into a cesspit to rot. Askobert also met a wretched end.

Kenelm's body came home to Winchcombe to lie with the bones of his father, Kenwulf, and from that time many miracles have been attributed him, notably those of healing the sick and the blind. A shrine for the holy body was built at the Abbey, a chapel at Sudeley, and a church by the spring that arose at Clent. In 985 AD, Oswald, Bishop of Worcester, rebuilt Winchcombe Abbey and rededicated it to the Virgin Mary and St. Kenelm.

Historical documents confirm that Kenelm was indeed the son of King Kenwulf but that most probably he died, perhaps in battle, before his father. His place of burial was at Winchcombe Abbey, which had been founded by Kenwulf c.798, and which became one of the largest landowners in the Cotswolds. In 1815 two sarcophagi were discovered at the eastern end of the ruined Abbey which were believed to be those of Kenelm and Kenwulf; they are preserved in St. Peter's church and now believed to date from the thirteenth century. But what of the legend? This appears to have originated here as the invention of an eleventh-century monk, and was repeated and widely publicised in the twelfth century by the chronicler William of Malmesbury. However, even without any evidential corroboration, in medieval England Kenelm came to be venerated as a saint and martyr, being mentioned by Chaucer in the *'Canterbury Tales'*. His tomb became an important shrine, attracting pilgrim's throughout the Middle Ages - perhaps the original reason for the elaboration of the legend.

STANWAY

Location On the B4077, three miles north-east of Winchcombe. Sheet 150 06073238

How many country houses can be said to have changed hands only once since the the eighth century, and that once from being monastic to domestic ownership? Stanway was a manor given to Tewkesbury Abbey on its foundation in 715 as sole endowment by a pair of Saxon brothers, of whom nothing is known beyond the curiosity of their names, Odo and Dodo. This was long before Gloucestershire contained more abbeys than any other county in England and from whence arose the saying *'As sure as God's in Gloucestershire'*. Then, four monks resided here in what cannot have been more than a cell, praying for the souls of their benefactors. Later the Abbots of Tewkesbury used the manor as a summer retreat.

Stanway was one of the first monastic establishments to be dissolved in Henry VIII's reign. The Tracy family of nearby Toddington had kept a predatory eye on the monks' properties in the neighbourhood, including Winchcombe and Hailes abbeys. Sir William Tracy, puritanical by nature, anti-clerical in politics and a friend of William Tyndale, had a second son, Sir Richard, to whom a lease over Stanway was granted in 1533, and following the dissolution a few years later purchased the freehold. Richard was as radical as his father and played a considerable part in the dismantling of Hailes Abbey, actually seizing the greatly venerated vessel containing the Holy Blood of Christ. These Tracys were a godless and fierce breed, directly descended from William Tracy, one of the four knights who left Thomas a Becket hacked to pieces in Canterbury Cathedral. Legend maintains that his horse's hooves are heard clattering on the road on each anniversary of the knight's death in search of a priest to shrive his soul, though why Stanway where he never lived was chosen has not been explained. No wonder the family were referred to by local people as *'The Tracys, the Tracys, the wind in their faces'*, on whose successors a curse was laid by the dispossessed clerics of Stanway. Clearly these Tracys were a colourful crowd for amongst their number were a pirate and a heretic whose body was exhumed and burnt at the stake.

However reprehensible the part played by the Tracys in the destruction of two monasteries, their successors did not lack an aesthetic perspective. The mansions they built at Hailes (long ago demolished) and Stanway bear witness to their architectural taste. Sir Richard however seems to have been too busy compiling anti-papistic tracts and combating superstitious abuses to engage in building. He was content to reside in the Abbot's *'fair stone house'*, or what remained of it at Stanway. In 1569 he was succeeded by his son Paul, created baronet in 1611, of less fanatical metal than his father and grandfather and builder of the west front of the house facing the churchyard, from which it is best seen.

The long front under four well-spaced and pointed gables with the immensely high sixty-light oriel at the south end is of regular, if severe design. It ante-dates the gatehouse, by which one approaches it at a right-angle and which, with the north arch, forms a forecourt. The gatehouse must date from James I's reign because Sir Paul died in 1620, being succeeded by another Sir Richard who died in 1637. Apparently also concerned to make his mark on the house, it is probably to him that we owe the imaginative splendour of the gatehouse and the south front. Coscombe quarry, on the top of the escarpment above Stanway, produces Yellow Guiting stone, which mellows into a rich golden colour. Stanway House, at the foot of the ancient *stane* or *stoney way,* is built of this glorious stone.

The exquisite, ornate gateway is a curious mixture of late Gothic and renaissance motifs. The more one looks at its curvilinear gables, projecting bay windows, filigree balustrading and Mannerist centre-piece of fluted columns, broken pediment bearing a box-like panel with coat-of-arms, outsize scallop-shells (the Tracy crest) and pointed entrance, the more mongrel it appears. The north arch seen through the gatehouse is by comparison almost pure Baroque in its rustication, broken scrolled pediment and niches. The two are undoubtedly contemporary and were perhaps designed by Timothy Strong, owner of the famous quarries at Little Barrington and Taynton, and founder of a dynasty of master-masons, rather than by Inigo Jones to whom it was once attributed on the grounds of its stylistic appearance.

The pyramid on Lidcombe Hill above the house is even more remarkable. Probably the largest in the British Isles, sixty feet high and standing on an open arched base, it formed the centrepiece of cascades and water-gardens which tumbled down the hill over ramps into a canal or lake. The belvedere's architect is unknown but a plaque records that it was built in 1750 by Robert Tracy, gentleman, (1706-67), in memory of his father. As the elder of identical twins, Robert had inherited the Tracy estates and it may be that his building of this pyramid was a way of thanking his father for his own good fortune. Robert became an MP and so alike were the brothers that to distinguish him from his twin John Tracy (later Atkyns, later Keck, 1706-73) as children, the elder had to wear a red ribbon tied round his waist. The last surviving member of the original family, Susan Tracy-Keck, whose father  was killed in a duel in Hyde Park in 1767, married the eighth Earl of Wemyss.

The high-level canal no longer exists but recently the cascade steps have been excavated with a view to bringing it back into operation.

The siting of the pyramid was indeed fortuitous, for it affords lovely views of the villages of Oxenton, Alderton and Dumbleton, of Bredon Hill, of the Malverns further away, and the distant Black Mountains of Wales.

CHIPPING CAMPDEN

The East Banqueting House exists because a wealthy seventeenth-century landowner felt the need for a folly to which

> *the family came at the end of the main meal, to drink rare wines and*
> *eat small cakes and sweet-meats.*

Having a building set aside for nothing more serious than post-prandial pleasure must be about as nonchalant as you can get.

Sir Baptist Hicks purchased the manor of Campden in or about 1609 from Anthony Smith, whose family had held it since the Reformation. Hicks came of a Gloucestershire family who were established as merchants in London, and he himself continued the family business of mercer, blending it with financial interests and moneylending on an increasing scale. Under James I and Charles I he had considerable dealings with the Crown, and an indication of his material success is given by the fact that each of his two daughters carried a dowry of £100,000. This wealth and usefulness to the Crown ensured access to the highest circles of influence and taste, aided further by the position of his brother as an intimate friend of Robert Cecil, Earl of Salisbury; undoubtedly Sir Baptist must have been familiar with projects such as the splendid house and garden that Lord Salisbury created at Hatfield before 1612.

Building evolved as one of Hicks's preoccupations in the first decade of the seventeenth century. In London he built Hicks Hall at Clerkenwell and began a palatial suburban residence, Campden House at Kensington. In 1612, only a few years after acquiring the manor, he plunged into a number of projects at Chipping Campden, including the almshouses in Church Street, and the creation of the town's water supply.

The estate at this time offered nothing like a grand residence, for the previous owners had lived in a small manor house at Combe, south-west of the town. Hicks's project to build a magnificent new mansion on land beside the church at Chipping Campden is thought to have begun as early as 1613. This new building was intended as a reflection of his vast wealth, and it is reputed to have cost £29,000 to build and £15,000 to furnish, both colossal sums for those days. One reason why the cost was so high may be that Sir Baptist feared he would not live to see the house finished, and hurried building on; for the same reason it is likely that the garden was formed concurrently with the building of the house, around 1613-20. In fact Sir Baptist survived until a year after his ennoblement as Viscount Campden in 1628. His widow lived on at Campden until 1643, but the estates passed to his son-in-law, Edward, Lord Noel, who was killed in the Royalist defence of Oxford. Two years later, in 1645, Royalist troops who had been garrisoning Campden Manor destroyed it on their retreat: ' ... *the house which was so faire, burnt ...*', as one account records. Sir Baptist's daughter, Lady Juliana Noel, continued to stay at Campden from time to time after the fire, and one tradition asserts that she used a part of the main house that had not been destroyed. After her death in 1680 at the age of 95, however, the ruins of the house quickly became a stone quarry for the townspeople, and only a fragment of the main, south facade of the house itself now survives; a forlorn crag of masonry with some windows and part of a doorway.

More survives of the other buildings associated with the mansion. The stables were converted after the Restoration into a house for the estate steward, now known as the Court House, while the building called 'the almonry' is named on the drawings as the laundry; but the most important survivals are undoubtedly the ornate gateway and the little pepper-pot lodges and the two splendid banqueting houses. Here can be recaptured something of the splendour Campden House must once have displayed. A riot of pinnacles and gables, the banqueting houses stand at either end of the terrace in front of the main facade of the house. Their arched openings were once longer, so they were more like open loggias than little houses. The lower parts, now solid, had elaborate balustrading, though at some date, possibly when they were turned into cottages, new pieces of stone were cut exactly to fit the gaps. The skyline of the banqueting houses displays an elaborate range of obelisks and strapwork cresting, and the chimneys have open, flame-like finials. The most poignant reminders of the vanished elegance of these enchanting little buildings are, however, the fragments of robust yet naive plaster frieze which remain in the upper room of the west banqueting house.

East Banqueting House

The banqueting houses were also features in the garden design, the layout now manifest as a series of earthworks south of the house. They show that here Chipping Campden possessed a hitherto unknown Mannerist garden with terraces, mounds and water features in many respects a copy of ideas used at Hatfield in the years before 1612.

Nearby, the tradition has been continued. A modern folly was built in the 1960s by Sir Gordon Russell, in the garden of his house at Kingcombe. It is a very small-scale, moated, sham castle with external stairs. Underneath is a tiny grotto with a kitchen, a secret passage, two hiding places, and sound effects.

CHIPPING NORTON

Location On the A44, fifteen miles east of Broadway. Sheet 164   30482679

Chipping Norton is the highest town in Oxfordshire, situated on the western slopes of a hillside that was once the site of a Norman castle. Norton gained its Chipping, the medieval term for market, itself derived from the Old English *ceapen,* in the time of King John, and evolved as a typical wool town with the traditional Perpendicular-style church as witness to its piety and prosperity. It is still an important market town but, like Cirencester, Northleach, Chipping Campden and others, no longer has the trade in wool and cloth that made it famous. Unlike these, however, Chipping Norton lasted until relatively recently as a cloth-manufacturing centre, if much reduced from former glories. One contributor to this lies in the valley on the outskirts to the south-west of the town: Bliss and Sons Tweed Mill is a Lancashire factory with an Italianate chimney set in the Oxfordshire Cotswold countryside, built in 1872 and operating continuously until it closed in 1982. By most definitions of follies, this utilitarian purpose excludes it from candidacy but the explorer who, seeing the mill for the first time, does not have his attention distracted by it is blind to the delights of architecture and the whimsicality of owners - distracted generally because there is a factory here at all, but more particularly by the odd-shaped dome from which rises the 'campanile' chimney of the mill.

There is quite a romance about this mill. It had its beginnings some two hundred years ago when Thomas Bliss started in business on his own account and quickly became known for the very fine quality of the cloths he manufactured. Bliss's father was a cloth manufacturer who operated from Chalford, a descendant of the Huguenots driven by religious persecution from the Low Countries in the sixteenth century who brought their skills in weaving and cloth-making to the valleys around Stroud. It was the task of young Bliss to carry his father's samples round the Cotswold towns: on one of his trips to Chipping Norton he met, fell in love with and subsequently married the daughter of the landlord of the Swan Inn. Liking young Bliss, his father-in-law purchased for him a small manufactury specialising in *tilts* for covering carts, light woollen *linseys* for women's petticoats, and *rugging* for horses.

This first business was conducted from, of all places, the Vicarage, the yarn being spun on spinning wheels of the cottages of Chipping Norton and surrounding villages. With the whole family (there were ten in all) and the women of the district assisting this family concern, trade increased rapidly. First, it was moved to a malt-house, then a nearby flour mill was added, but this had the drawback of being dependent upon water for power - there was no water for four months of the year and in a dry season it was even longer. By now, horse clothing had become a speciality and was supplied direct to the Royal Stables at Buckingham Palace. Still everything was being cut by old hand shears which were sent to Nailsworth once a year for sharpening!

In 1816, William Bliss (the second generation) retired through ill-health and his fourteen-year-old son, Robert, took over the management of the business instead of continuing at school. Eight years later Robert emigrated to America, leaving an aunt in charge, and there was considerable surprise in Chipping Norton when after six years he returned with an American bride.

In 1839, William Bliss, the second of that name, took over the mill and it was he who had the greatest impact on its fortunes. Records show that the weekly wage bill at the commencement of his management was £17, but thirty-eight years later it had risen to £500. The mill was enlarged and turnover increased out of all proportion to its humble beginnings. In 1851, at the Great Exhibition, the firm was awarded two First Class Medals for shawls and for tweeds. Success bred success, and at the exhibitions in New York and Paris, Royal Awards were gained by the firm. In 1867, William Bliss, an Englishman, was awarded the French Emperor's prize of £500 for the employer who had done most to promote the welfare of his work people.

Calamity followed. In 1872, in the space of two hours, fire destroyed most of the mill. Refusing to be beaten, however, a new mill - to be the best ever built, the most ornamental, and completely fireproof - was ordered, designed and erected within twelve months, and not a piece of the old building was used in the construction. It was designed by the Lancashire architect, George Woodhouse, in the style of a French chateau, with balustraded parapets punctuated by graceful urns, apparently to blend in with the rural location. Industrial chimneys do seem to bring out the eccentric in mill owners. Here the imposition of a single gigantic Tuscan factory chimney erupting out of the central domed bay front to twice the height of the building, is visually very effective. Sticking out of the middle of the building like a candle on a cake, it rises to 165 feet. One can only stop and wonder at such obtrusive camouflage, even if it is listed Grade II*. The dome, whose parapet is sixty-four feet from the ground, often arouses curiosity and was an integral part of the new building: it is so planned that a stairway runs round inside it. There was a bell fixed at dome level to ring the times of working hours; and still keeping ahead, the mill was the first in Britain to be run by electricity.

The mill has been converted to luxury flats but gives the residents the tallest television aerial in the Cotswolds.

RADWAY

Of the shires, Warwickshire probably has the fewest follies, which is surprising when one considers that here was the home county of Sanderson Miller, one of the most influential folly-builders in Britain. His name is met frequently when researching the designers of follies: some trick of fame and the size of his constructions preserve his memory even while the names of more inventive designers are lost to us. He was also, at the beginning, an amateur: the English love amateurs, employ them wherever possible, and then seem reluctant to pay them!

Miller was born in 1716 at Radway Grange under the lee of Edge Hill, the son of a prosperous Banbury mercer. At 21 he inherited from his father a substantial fortune which enabled him to lead the life of a gentleman-architect, together with the Grange, the grounds of which he immediately began to improve with fountains and cascades. In 1744 he erected his first building, the picturesque Thatched Cottage, which attracted favourable comment from Dean Jonathon Swift, and a year later began to Gothicise the fronts of the sixteenth-century Grange, a full six years before anyone else in the country.

Miller completed his first major folly between 1747 and 1750. Radway Tower, or Castle, was sensationally received by society for its positioning and its apparent authenticity. Built on the spot where King Charles I was supposed to have raised his standard before the indecisive battle, it commanded a magnificent sweeping view to the north-west, but architectually appears to have been based on Guy's Tower at Warwick Castle, with thin, almost fragile castellations surmounting stumpy little machicolations. Judged by the standard of other folly-towers this one appears common-place - but it is a seminal folly by a master folly-builder.

All the work is in yellow free-stone. On one side of the path is the sham ruin of a large arch, and opposite is the entrance to the Tower. This must once have had two fat square castellated towers flanking the gate, but now the right-hand one is sawn off at an angle and has a roof and chimney. Through the gate an immovable stone draw-bridge crosses to the *'lofty octagonal tower'*. It is now a public house, but the picnic room, with pretty plasterwork and elegant windows and niches, remains empty. The Bishop of Ossory visited the Castle in 1756, writing

> *...in one of these niches is to be placed Caractacus in chains,*
> *modelled, under Mr Miller's directions, by a countryman of*
> *great genius now established in London.*

But, when finished, Caractacus was too big for the niche and had to go in the garden.

An indication of how Miller's contemporaries reacted to his style is given in Richard Jago's 1767 poem, *'Edge Hill, or the Rural Prospect delineated and moralised'*:

14

Thanks Miller! To thy paths
That ease our winding steps! Thanks to the fount,
The trees, the flowers, imparting to the sense
Fragrance, or ducet sound of murmuring rill,
And stilling ev'ry tumult in the breast!
And oft the stately wood, and oft the broken arch,
Or mould'ring wall, well taught to counterfeit
The waste of time, to solemn thought excite,
And crown with graceful pomp a shaggy hill.

Somewhat eccentric, and a noted party-giver, Miller is said to be the model for Squire Ashworth in Fielding's *Tom Jones*. In later years he suffered from bouts of insanity and was treated by the same physician as George III.

Radway Tower

Sanderson Miller was a trend-setter rather than a technician, a pioneer of the eighteenth-century Gothic revival; his charm, sociability and avant-garde taste won him fashionable friends and commissions which were drawn up as often as not by his master mason, William Hitchcox. The combination of Miller's ideas and romantic imagination was unbeatable: to have him design you a castle stained, in Horace Walpole's famous phrase, with *'the true rust of the Baron's Wars'* was to be in the height of fashion. Here at Radway, Sanderson Miller had originated a style of ruined castle which in its various forms was to be imitated the length and breadth of Britain. Whether he tired of improving his own estate or found more enjoyment in new challenges we do not know, but Miller built nothing else at Radway.

WALTON

Location Off the A429, four miles east of Stratford-on-Avon. Sheet 151 28525242

Long ago, the hamlet of Walton consisted of two manors, Walton D'Eiville and Walton Mauduit. Before that, the Romans knew it too, for it is less than a mile away from the Fosse Way, and they may even have had a villa here. On the slopes of Bath Hill, almost secluded by trees, is the Bath House. With the reputation the Romans had for constructing baths in many parts of the country, they may have built one here, for the lower half of the building is ancient. The current Bath House is a hexagonal building designed by the eighteenth-century gentleman architect Sanderson Miller as a summer *'destination'* in the woodland grounds of the Walton estate.

On the ground floor it consists of one room with shells festooning the walls, plasterwork icicles hanging from the domed ceiling, and an open fire. A basement grotto contains a plunge pool fed by seven chilly freshwater springs, which tumble over stone and fern with the pleasant music of a waterfall.

IDLICOTE

Location Off the A429, seven miles south-east of Stratford. Sheet 151 28394432

In the grounds of Idlicote House is an unusually large, tall octagonal structure, built of white stone embellished with red Kenilworth dressing stones. The parapet is embattled and the roof is pointed. An upper window on the west side has mullions, but the ogee windows on the sides of the other walls are relatively modern. There are large fascial decorations in the form of cross loops. But what is it? Little of the masonry appears to be ancient, so is it a comparatively modern rebuild of something? Was it originally from Kenilworth Abbey where it may have been, at least in part, a dovecote? Certainly the estate was owned by the Abbey until its dissolution in 1539, but was it really moved by the monks to provide meat for the holy brothers?

17

FARNBOROUGH

Location Six miles north of Banbury, half a mile west of A423. Sheet 151 43024903

At Farnborough Park five very different, elegant structures were built, all complementing each other: three along a great elevated terrace, a game larder reached by a path on the return to the house, but the fifth, a pentagon summer-house with balcony, has not survived.

The Terrace Walk of 1751, a grassed and curving walk giving spectacular views over and above the great plain of Warwickshire, rises gently from the south front of the house, along the ridge, past two classical temples, and culminates after three-quarters of a mile at an obelisk; semi-circular grass 'platforms' project the viewer into the surrounding countryside. It has often been compared with the Terrace at Rievaulx in Yorkshire, for they are two of the most ambitious landscaping projects of their kind. and both are tributes to the *Picturesque* movement, with which William Holbech of Farnborough Hall and his neighbour, Sanderson Miller, the gentleman-architect of Radway, were closely allied.

The Oval Pavilion, was built some six decades earlier, soon after the Holbech family took possession of the property in 1684. Sometimes called the Prospect Tower, this Pavilion, together with the Ionic Temple, has generally been attributed to Miller, who was also advising Lord Lyttelton at Hagley during that same period. It is formed of an open loggia with four Tuscan columns around a stone table, with an outside stone staircase at the rear that leads up to a room of extraordinary beauty. Its domed ceiling and curved walls are decorated with plaster rocaille, probably by the Yorkshire master of stucco, William Perritt, who executed the similar decoration in the house.

The eighteenth-century game larder, its temperature controlled by louvres still operational through a system of pulleys, is thought to be to the design of Sanderson Miller.

Oval Pavilion

Game Larder

SEZINCOTE

Sezincote is an experience not a village, for the mansion and gardens are north India come to the Cotswolds. It impresses because it comes as such a surprise. In ruins it would, unhesitatingly, be described as a folly: as a well-cared for country house it can best be described as most eccentric. Sezincote is unique, thought to be the only Moghul building to have survived in western Europe, located on a broad, sloping hillside surrounded by parkland where cedars and other foreign trees have grown into mature and splendid beauty, and where a willow-hung lake provides a haven for native water-fowl. Its oddity, its domed roof once burnished copper but now coated with verdigris, and Indian imagery expresses its originator's determination to show at all costs that he was no ordinary gentleman.

Sezincote derives its name from the Old English *cisen,* meaning gravelly, and though less poetical is certainly less conjectural than Sir Robert Atkyns's derivation, viz. *seisin* from *chesne,* meaning an oak, and *coed,* a wood. Atkyns did not describe the house he found there in his eighteenth-century *History of Glostershire.* Instead he dwelt upon the dreadful iniquity of the Elizabethan owner of the manor, Ludovic Grevill, who was involved in a plot to kill his former servant, forge his will and inherit the money - but was discovered and hanged, instead! Neither Ludovic Grevill nor Sir Robert in their wildest dreams can have imagined the Sezincote which centuries later was to arise like an oriental exhalation out of the Cotswold escarpment.

It was in 1795 that John Cockerell, a Colonel in the East India Company's service at Bengal and at one time Quartermaster-General to Lord Cornwallis, bought Sezincote from the third Earl of Guildford. Like so many others, Cockerell had made a fortune by exploiting his position. The Sezincote estate may have been found for him by his friend Warren Hastings, the former Governor General of Bengal, whose house at nearby Daylesford was just being completed to the designs of John Cockerell's brother, Samuel Pepys Cockerell. As soon as the estate was in his hands, Colonel Cockerell began busying himself with plans for alterations to the house and the creation of a garden. Building work was certainly in progress during 1798 but shortly afterwards proceedings were brought to an abrupt halt by his sudden death.

In his will Cockerell left Sezincote equally to his brothers, Charles and Samuel, and his married sister. Charles, who had also made a fortune on his own account as an executive of the East India Company, and was to become a baronet in 1809 and Member of Parliament for Evesham, agreed to buy out the interest of the other two. Work did not, however, resume on John Cockerell's modest remodelling of the old house: Charles had grander plans. Together with his brother, an architect of some standing who had been surveyor to the East India Company, and his friends, Thomas and William Daniell, uncle and nephew who had just returned from ten years' travelling in India, he had conceived the conceit of conjuring India into the Cotswolds, of so dressing up an English house and garden as to remind him of his Indian past. The scheme was carried forward with Samuel as architect and the Daniells as specialist consultants, supplying ideas for decorative details from their store of Indian drawings.

Work began about 1805, for in April of that year Edward Clarke of Witney, mason, gave prices for building the house amounting to just under £6,000. By 1813 he had received £6,789, and his refusal to refund the surplus led eventually to a lawsuit. These sums must refer only to the building of the shell of the house and conservatory: the style of the interior suggests that work continued until c.1820.

The house itself is low, simulating a bungalow, with lightly raised roofs. Until one looks closely into the detail one's attention is rivetted upon the ethereal onion-shaped dome, floating upon its centre and pointing to the skies with a long spiky finial. The dome rides upon a square platform poised upon a rather squat tower. One of Samuel Cockerell's first designs for the house included no fewer than five domes of equal size but this was modified. The oriental effect does not depend solely upon the dome, however. At the far corners of the tower are slim *chattris*. The skyline is a perplexing medley of these minaret-like features, some of which are made of copper. The pronounced, broad, bracketed *chujjah*, or cornice, enhances the Indian effect, as does the

pointed entrance arch reaching to the top of the upper storey, and the hooded windows.

The extraordinary golden-orange glow of the stone heightens the effect: the stone from the quarry above Bourton-on-the-Hill is not naturally that colour and to increase the fantasy of the building and authenticate the colour of its material, the native stone was stained artificially to impart a more Indian orange tone.

A formal garden with soaring Irish yews is overlooked to the south by a grand, sweeping, concave conservatory, the Orangery, with minarets, ending in an octagonal room, while to the north a curved passage, fronted with iron trellis work ends in an octagonal domed pavilion with high Moorish windows, decorated to resemble a tent with wooden spears supporting a canopy. This once served as Sir Charles's tent bedroom but disintegrated several years ago and the spears which held up the roof have been incorporated into an immense slate bed, now in the main block.

The ornament of the house is Moghul rather than Hindu style and it is extraordinary that these Moghul ornaments, pinnacles and pots were all carved by native Cotswold masons. Perhaps its design strength is that the house appears though a compromise between the Cockerell brothers' Indian interests and contemporary ideas of an English gentleman's house, plus a few concessions to western European climate: the pungent orientalism of Sezincote is a dress with which a late-Georgian Classical house has been clothed. Classicism is visible in the symmetry of the elevations and the lifting of the main rooms to a first-floor *piano nobile,* but stylistic interaction is evident everywhere. Its large round-headed windows, neo-classical in proportion, are embellished with decoration of Eastern origin; the onion-shaped dome rises between chimney-stacks that despite attempts to give them hints of the Orient persist in being chimney-stacks.

It is the mixture of Hindu and Muslim detail which makes Sezincote a unique example of the architecture of Akbar, the best-known of the Moghuls rulers from 1556 to 1605, who deliberately mixed Islamic and Hindu elements in architecture in an effort to integrate culturally the diverse country that his ancestors had conquered. The pillars and horizontal beam over the front door are of Hindu inspiration, as are the many representations of the lotus, whereas the chattris and the chujjah are Muslim. The 'peacock tail' arches crowning the first floor windows can be seen often in Rajasthan, where the Moghuls built their main palaces, but the dome, a characteristic of Muslim architecture representing heart and heaven - a symbol of peace and tranquility - shows the Persian influence.

Inside, the house is contemporary, for the decoration is not Indian but classical Greek Revival. From its completion, Sezincote attracted attention. The Revd. F E Witts, Rector of Upper Slaughter, recorded in his diary:

> *August 30th, 1828. Made a little excursion to Sezincote, where we passed nearly two hours in viewing the house and grounds. The exterior of the former is striking and picturesque, after a Hindu model, the tomb of Hyder Ali, and the first view of the house, conservatory, flower garden, bank of wood, etc., very peculiar and pleasing; but the interior is badly arranged, and not particularly well-furnished. Several new apartments for bed-chambers have recently been added; but the situation is very unfavourable under a high bank of clay covered with dense foliage, hence the house, conservatory and offices are very damp and the dry rot has already commenced its ravages. The shrubberies and drest grounds are pretty and peculiar, the oriental taste is preserved, as far as it could ... Sir Charles and Lady Cockerell are now abroad.*

If the house was conceived in 1805, then the gardens were begun before building started. Here the Indian theme is more thoroughgoing, for which Thomas Daniell was directly responsible. The Daniells worked in concert with Humphrey Repton, to whom the park and lake below the house were entrusted in 1804, and whose delightfully landscaped garden has trees of enormous size. Even if *sezincote* does not mean *hillside of the oaks,* oaks are plentiful in the acres of surrounding parkland; old woodland spreads all around studded with ornamental trees, which contrast wierdly with the exotic architecture. The extent of Repton's involvement

21

in the planting and layout is not known precisely. Certainly he never produced a 'Red Book' of Sezincote as he did for most of his other great landscaping works, but there exists a sketch with overlay drawn by him which shows his ideas for the south garden, and he mentioned his work here in several of his writings.

Now, beautiful gardens surround a stream, watered by a copious spring on the steep hill, which curves away from the house downhill to a pool. The Daniells' Indian layout soon confronts the visitor for the drive to the house crosses an Indian Bridge spanning a dell, the cast-iron octagonal columns copied from the Elephanta Caves, its balustrade surmounted by sacred, crouching Brahmin bulls. That Sir Charles took deep interest in the whole project can be seen from a letter he wrote to Thomas Daniell insisting that both bulls on the bridge be retained:

> *I am dreadfully alarmed about the Brahmin Bulls - because I am certain they cannot be better placed - could Viswakarma, the Artist of the Gods of the Hindoos, take a peep at Sezincote, he would say let the bulls remain where they are.*

All the Brahmin bulls - by the Temple, on the Bridge and in front of the Orangery - are Nandi, 'the happy one', Shiva's favourite. Originally made of Coade stone, they were disintegrating so badly that a model was taken of the least affected and they are cast in iron.

The Temple Pool shows the figure of Souriya, the Hindu sun goddess, occupying a small Indian shrine with a stepped pyramid roof, also designed by Daniell, at the head of the little valley. Souriya features, drawn by seven swift horses, in the Hindu Vedas, the oldest religious text in the world. Although a relatively minor god, she is prayed to to stimulate the intellect of the worshipper.

Below the bridge is the Snake Pool where a three-headed snake or serpent coils round a tree trunk and spouts water from its mouths. Below that again is the Island Pool. Particularly clever is the choice of English plants arranged to give an oriental appearance, seen to best advantage in subdued light - few gardens can look so attractive in the rain. The South Garden, with canals and rows of Irish yews, copies the traditional 'Paradise Garden' much used by

Babur, the first Moghul. The canals or paths dividing the garden into four equal parts represent the four rivers of life and their crossing is a symbol of the meeting of humanity and God. The octagon shape (the fountain, Pavilion, etc) evolved from the squaring of a circle, reconciling the material side of man (Square) with eternity (circle).

So impressed was Repton with the Daniells' landscaping of the ravine and so enthusiastic about the *'new sources of beauty and variety'* offered by Indian architecture that he prevailed upon the Prince of Wales, then Prince Regent, to visit to Sezincote in 1807. The Prince was captivated, and from that visit sprang the project to model the Pavilion at Brighton on the Indian style, although Nash, not Cockerell, Repton or Daniell, was entrusted with the main task there.

Temple of Souriya

Sir Charles did not live long after completion of his house. He died in 1837 and was succeeded by his son Charles, who on the expectation of inheriting Northwick Park through his mother Harriet Rushout, a daughter of the 1st Lord Northwick, changed his name to Rushout. But when the last Lord Northwick died in 1887 that estate, owing to some slip of a solicitor's pen, went to Lord Edward Spencer-Churchill by mistake. The expense of a prolonged lawsuit resulted in Sir Charles Rushout having to sell Sezincote, for he lost everything in unsuccessful legal moves to gain possession. In 1888 Sezincote was acquired by James Dugdale, from Lancashire, whose grandson, John, became a friend of John Betjeman and who was a frequent visitor from Oxford: no description conjures up the flavour of the old Sezincote more nostalgically than that in his poem, *Summoned by Bells.*

Snake Pool

Inside the Conservatory

23

BATSFORD

> *On Christmas Day Lord and Lady Redesdale with some young people*
> *were playing at Snap Dragon but having unfortunately put the Raisins*
> *into the Spirits of Wine instead of Brandy, the Raisins bounced about*
> *and three ladies were set in a blaze, two were burnt most dreadfully*
> *and were obliged to keep their beds for many days.*

Surprisingly, these bright young people were not friends of the Mitford sisters about whom we read so much today, but of an earlier generation. The author of this passage was Miss Anne Rushout of neighbouring Northwick Park in her unpublished *Journal* of 1813, and the Lord Redesdale mentioned was Sir John Mitford (1748-1820), who had been made Speaker of the House of Commons 1801-02 in the place of Addington, and Lord Chancellor of Ireland 1802-06; on this latter appointment Sir John was created Lord Redesdale. He was not an easy man to get on with. His

> *integrity was unimpeachable, his manners were stiff, and his sense of*
> *humour was deficient.*

Batsford had been the seat of the Freeman family from 1490 but in 1808 Lord Redesdale inherited the estate of several thousand acres and a pleasant early-Georgian house from a rich and highly respected squire, Thomas Edwards-Freeman, the childless husband of Redesdale's mother's sister. The ostensible reason for the bequest was that Edwards-Freeman too had an ancestor, Richard, who had held the office of Lord Chancellor of Ireland, under Queen Anne. A supplementary reason was the manner in which Lord Redesdale's son won Edwards-Freeman's affection. One day the father took his little son to see Mr. Freeman who to amuse the child played for him on an old barrel organ. When the performance was over the child had said to his father, "Give the poor old man a shilling." In return for the inheritance of Batsford, Lord Redesdale was obliged to assume by royal licence the additional name and arms of Freeman.

In 1886 the estate was left to Algernon Bertram Freeman-Mitford, grandfather of the Mitford sisters, and who in 1902 was made by his great friend King Edward VII 1st Lord Redesdale of the second creation. Bertram or Bertie (pronounced *Bartie*) Mitford was handsome and cultivated. He moved in exclusive London circles and the Marlborough House set and in 1863 was sent as Second Secretary to the Embassy in St. Petersburg. The lure of the east captivated him and in 1886 he was transferred to Tokyo where he learned to speak Japanese and concluded some difficult negotiations with the Mikado. Of his several published books, the most famous was *Tales of Old Japan*. In between, from 1874 to 1886, he was appointed Secretary to the Board of Works, which brought him into even closer touch with the Prince of Wales. His many talents also brought him into association with the artists Whistler, Leighton and Milais, and with men of letters Carlyle and Edmund Gosse.

Between 1888 and 1892 Bertram Mitford built the present house. The style was entirely different to its predecessor and was dictated at a time of supreme confidence in the future of the English country house. Lord and Lady Redesdale held enormous house parties, and entertained King Edward VII here. However, Lord Ronald Leveson-Gower, staying in July, 1897, could find nothing more to say than,

> *The house is a very roomy and a most comfortable one, of no style in*
> *particular, with a large hall and a spacious dining-room. There are*
> *some family portraits, but the principal feature of this place is over a*
> *mile of wild garden.*

It amazed him that Sir Ernest Satow, Minister in Japan, and the Keeper of Kew Gardens were fellow guests. But Bertram Mitford was more interested in his garden than his house. Moreover, he had brought with him from his four years in Japan an admiration of the country which, with his newly-inherited estate and fortune, he had opportunity to translate into reality. A man as talented as Redesdale could have reached the top in any of his chosen fields but it is for his arboretum and his Japanese gardens that he will be best remembered. He created these largely under the influence of Sir Joseph Hooker, and went to considerable lengths to obtain oriental plants and shrubs. In another of his books, *The Bamboo Garden,* his enthusiasm for his subject was allowed to run rampant: so too in the garden for he planted no less than fifty species, brought from the Himalayas, China, Japan, and the United States.

Redesdale's enthusiasm both for trees and for Japan is manifest in The Japanese Rest House, a pretty red and white tea-house temple, set on a knoll among very fine trees, up four rough, rock steps, with bronze dragon-flies on each side; a third, smaller one is on the roof. The wide eaves of the roof of this square, red-brick building are supported on twelve pine trunks round the edge of a red tile platform. On each side of the door is a strip of Japanese characters extolling the virtues of bamboo - there are many clumps of it planted around but none was used in the construction. Inside, there is a white board ceiling, red brick walls and more red tiles for the floor; it is possible that the walls were once covered with silk or paper but this has long gone.

In the gardens there are other reminders of the Orient, a bronze Buddha, two bronze deer, and an animal like a veil-tailed Peke stuffed with tennis balls, his paws on a cloisonne ball.

Lord Redesdale's extravagance in building and gardening brought about a serious decline in his fortunes. In 1910 he was obliged to let the house and moved his family to Pont Street, London. After his eldest son Clement's death in the Great War he returned to Batsford for a short twilight period, but even then only part of the house was in use; the rest was under dustsheets. When he died in 1916 he was succeeded by his eldest surviving son David, also serving in the army. The 2nd Lord Redesdale and his wife lived in the big house for a few years with skeleton staff and the eldest of their growing family, Nancy, Pamela and Tom, were brought up here as small children in a happy and carefree manner, but in 1919 Lord Redesdale sold Batsford and moved to Swinbrook. The occupancy by the Freeman family had come to an end.

Bronze deer

Japanese Rest House finial

STOW-ON-THE-WOLD

Location On the A436 and A429. Sheet 163 20212563

Stow-on-the-Wold is situated on a high ridge, 800 feet above sea level between the valleys of the Evenlode and the Dikler, exposed to the unchecked winds that blow across the wolds. In the eighteenth century it was said, jokingly, that the town lacked earth, fire and water, but had plenty of air. Created at the intersection of eight roads in the time of Henry I, when it was known as Edwardstowe, it developed into a major market town, as its spacious square testifies.

Although there is nothing of outstanding size, there are a number of small, almost intimate follies in the town. Along Oxford Road can be found Enoch's Tower of 1848, a castellated folly four storeys tall, so-called because it is where a Mr Enoch kept an unofficial museum of local material. The Tower has since been converted into a house.

Enoch's Tower

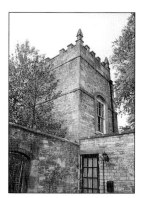

Fossway House

In the garden of Fossway House is a folly with an embattled, pinnacled tower like a small church, built of rubble, with an ashlar parapet and quoins. This, too, is now used as a house.

East of the Fosse Way a romantic pleasure garden was built about 1800, which presented a wooded walk passing under the road from Maugersbury, through a tunnel and down to St. Edward's Well. A derelict classical cottage lies in trees near a small artificial pond and stream, and there are also paths and a grotto higher up on the west side of the main road in the grounds of Quarwood, the great Gothic house built in 1857 but altered beyond recognition in 1954. All that remains of the original designs are the Gothic stone gateposts.

Grotto, Quarwood

SHERBORNE

Turn south off the former coaching road between Oxford and Cheltenham, now the A40, west of Burford and east of Northleach, and you will find yourself on a narrow, straight lane apparently bound for nowhere. The wolds over which you pass hold little attraction, but do persevere until the trees of Larkethill Wood loom on your right. Suddenly, without warning, you will get a glimpse of a breath-taking little building set behind a forecourt, guarded by a pair of low lodges. These latter were built in 1898 but the house they serve dates from two-and-a-half centuries earlier, during the Protectorate. It was built for John Dutton, grandson of Thomas Dutton who had bought the Sherborne Park estate exactly a hundred years previously.

The manor of Sherborne belonged in the Middle Ages to the Abbots of Winchcombe, and by tradition they had a manor house on the site of Sherborne House. During the reign of Henry VIII a London merchant, Sir John Alleyn, obtained a lease of the property, and following dissolution of the Abbey he purchased the freehold. In 1551, however, his son, Christopher, sold Sherborne to Thomas Dutton, and the Duttons remained here for four centuries, becoming one of Gloucestershire's leading families.

In spite of his physical disability caused by a spinal deformity, and called 'Crump' because of his hunchback, Sir John Dutton was an engaging and picturesque figure, and emerges from the Civil War era as one of the more sympathetic figures on the political stage. There were not many soldiers in those Wars who on the one hand fought as Cavaliers on behalf of the King, with whom 'Crump' was at the battle of Oxford and offered to lend as much as £50,000, and had to be dissuaded from further military service because of his disability, yet on the other became such a close personal friend of Oliver Cromwell that they considered arranging the marriage together of their two eldest children, Cromwell's daughter and Dutton's son. He was also, according to his contemporary Anthony a Wood,

> *a learned and prudent man, and as one of the richest, so one of the*
> *meekest men in England.*

He was certainly one of the richest, for he could ride from Sherborne to Cheltenham without leaving his own land; as to being prudent, that is doubtful for he was an inveterate gambler and on one occasion put up his whole estate on a single bet, only to be saved by his manservant forcibly dragging him from the gaming table after being startled into action by the cry, 'Sherborne's up, Sherborne's up'. Despite his great wealth, through his friendship with Cromwell Sir John was able to avoid the severest consequences of his royal allegiance, and his composition fines amounted to only some £6,000. He was therefore clearly in a position to build during the years of the Protectorate.

A house of substance suitable for the reception of the royal court existed at Sherborne, for Queen Elizabeth visited Thomas Dutton here in 1574, staying six days, and she came again to stay with his son in 1592. It is not known how far this was replaced in the mid-seventeenth century rebuilding by 'Crump', but certainly one of his major projects was the creation of a new hunting park and erection of a lodge. A park had existed at Sherborne in the late sixteenth century, represented today by the 'Home Park', lying between the house and the A40.

'Crump's 'New Park' lay much further south, on land partly in the parish of Aldsworth, and reputed to have been laid out between 1624 and 1640.

Though it has been regarded as one of the most perfect small houses in England, he did not build Lodge Park to live in, for his residence was still Sherborne House, on the lush banks of Sherborne Brook. Lodge Park was erected as a standing or viewing-place or grandstand from the flat roof of which 'Crump', his family and his friends could watch stag- and deer-coursing by greyhounds along the arrow-straight landscape of exactly a mile. In 1655, Oliver Cromwell signed a warrant allowing his friend John Dutton to stock his new Deer Park by taking bucks and does from the Royal Hunting Ground in Wychwood Forest. From the roof there are also splendid views over the surrounding countryside.

From the late seventeenth century to the present one, the design of Lodge Park has been ascribed to Inigo Jones and this is not difficult to understand - at a distance Lodge Park bears a certain resemblance to Jones's Whitehall Banqueting House in outline and fenestration. But architectural experts now deem the Jones attribution improbable. The highly-ornate facade is too old-fashioned and too cluttered for England's great Palladian architect, who actually died during the time the Lodge was being built. At first sight it may appear Classical but closer inspection reveals that its derivation is more French than Italian. Moreover, the rusticated porch arcades are Jacobean, as also are the shell niches between the closely packed windows of the first floor. These are made to sit on the segmental heads of the lower, in a rather uncouth manner. No less unorthodox are the double broken pediments of these windows all running together like a continuous string-course. The whole front is bristling with sculptural masks and devices and the topmost balustrade is most intricately carved.

If Jones had a connection, the design was more probably the work of John Webb, his chief pupil and assistant, but carried out with some variations by the local sculptor-master-mason, Valentine Strong. One suggestion is that its confusion of Classical and vernacular detail results from a local mason - quite possibly Strong - altering a purer design by John Webb. This, of course, only increases the difficulty of identifying the designer of what must now be admitted as a pioneering Classical building. If we accept that the rich mixture of Classical and vernacular influences is equally impossible for either Jones or a Cotswold man, who could be responsible? The only other person who seems at all probable is Nicholas Stone. He was principally a sculptor, but is known to have carried out some architectural work, and was in the Oxford area in 1632-33, building Cornbury Park and the gateways at the Oxford Botanic Garden. His client in both cases was the Earl of Danby, who owned the Cirencester Park estate until 1615, and could be expected to have known Dutton. Was Stone recommended to Dutton by Danby and at least provided the designs for Lodge Park, even if he did not carry them out? However, to compound the confusion Dutton's name does not appear in Stone's office notebook or accounts, which makes his involvement unlikely.

Now Valentine Strong is thought to be the designer and builder per se. It is a valid assumption. In the first place, he was a member of a family of prolific builders who owned the stone quarries at Little Barrington adjacent to Sherborne Park, and at Taynton nearby. Secondly, he is known to have extended Sherborne House for 'Crump' Dutton between 1651-53. Thirdly, the sculptor-mason could readily have derived his inspiration from the French pattern books of Du Cerceau and Philibert de L'Orme, which were *de rigeur* at the time.

But the matter is by no means settled and becomes more complex. In the past, a date in the 1650s has usually been assigned to the Lodge. However, a manuscript has recently come to light giving a clear description of the Lodge, made by a visitor c. 1634, viz:

> *...one stately, rich, compacted Building all of Free-stone, flat, and cover'd with Lead, with strong Battlements about not much unlike to that goodly, and magnificent Building the Banquetting House at Whitehall. This stately house is mounted on a High Hill, in the Champian, commaunding, and over-topping her owne Shire, and some neighbour Shires, adiacent, to her, plac'd with in a wall'd Parke, that is well stor'd with good Venison: This stately Lodge was lately built at the great Cost and Charges of a noble true hearted Gentleman, more for the pleasure of his worthy Friends, then his*

owne profit; Itt is richly furnish'd to entertaine them to see that Kingly sport, and pleasure, admirably perform'd, in that rare Paddocke course of a Mile in length, and walled on either Side. There I spent a full houre, with the good favour of the Keeper, in viewing that neat, rare Building, the rich furnish'd Roomes, the handsome contriv'd Pens and Places, where the Deere are kept, and turn'd out for the Course; and the manner, and order of the Paddock Sport.

Does this mean that the Lodge was built but the park not stocked for another two decades, even allowing for the turmoil of the Civil Wars in which 'Crump' was an active participant? Or did 'Crump' take advantage of his friendship with Cromwell to restock the park in 1655 with fresh, healthy deer, rather than this being an initial stocking? Or was there some other explanation?

Behind the ravishing little facade, Lodge Park consisted originally of only two rooms running the full length of the building: a hall on the ground floor and a banqueting room above, which led onto the balcony; both heated by imposing stone fireplaces on the back wall of the hall, each with a great stone overmantle in the shape of a shell. The staircase was a free-standing structure against the north wall, carried on carved wooden posts. The roof was used as a viewing platform for the deer coursing, access being gained by another staircase in the north-west corner.

Dutton did not expect to use Lodge Park exclusively. The grandstand, enclosure and beech spinney (which still survives, a mile away) from which the deer were 'slipped', could be used by anyone who would pay for the day's sport - the 'rules' required payment of half-a-crown per dog, and twelve pence to the 'slipper'.

In the early nineteenth century Lodge Park became two gamekeepers' cottages, until in 1898 Emily, Lady Sherborne, converted it into a dower house, which involved partitioning the two rooms and adding accommodation at the rear. After the last war Charles Dutton, seventh Lord Sherborne, moved out of Sherborne House and into Lodge Park and on his death without issue in 1982 left the whole estate to the National Trust.

WROXTON

The grounds of Wroxton Abbey were laid out between 1733 and 1748, possibly to his own design, by Lord North, later Earl of Guildford. The plan centred on two lakes, with a cascade and rocaille between them, and a serpentine river, using the gentle hills and the remaining ground with exceptional skill. This was then 'improved' with the addition of a number of novel buildings including a pretty obelisk and a Roman Doric temple. The obelisk, erected to commemorate a visit by the Prince of Wales during Banbury races in 1739, immediately draws the visitor's attention, but a formal lake lies in the way, possibly the remains of a layout by Tilleman Bobart in 1728 - the patte-d'oie abandoned, the lake kept. The obelisk is seen through a yew arch, and then one's interest is drawn to the left of the lake where a low bridge with two arches takes the path irresistibly on to the picturesque landscaping of the lakes themselves, with rushes, swans, yews, beeches, cedars and a low wall. A temple once stood on a mound between the lakes, possibly Sanderson Miller's *'Gothic open rotondo'* of 1750, which had protective curtains wound up and down on screws. Its protective belt of yews is still here. Here too were a Chinese summer house, bridge and shelter. Horace Walpole described the Chinoiserie - the first ever recorded - with which Wroxton's park was decorated:

> *There are several paltry Chinese buildings and bridges, which have the*
> *merit or demerit of being the progenitors of a very numerous race all*
> *through the kingdom; at least they were of the very first.*

Unfortunately, not a trace remains. They were, however, well used for a letter of July, 1749, survives, inviting

> *...if you think we shall escape a wet day tomorrow, I hope we shall have the*
> *pleasure of your company to cold meat and iced cream at the Chinese House.*

As well as the obelisk and the classical temple there is a dovecote trying to look like an ancient Gothick tower, but the real joy to be discovered is the Sanderson Miller eyecatcher of 1750, one of the most beautiful of all eyecatchers, superbly placed in front of beeches on its hilltop a mile away from the Abbey, south of Drayton. Such eyecatchers originated in the 'improving' movement of the eighteenth century with its related yearning for an ideal of the Middle Ages. When a landlord improved his estate with planting, clearing and the creation of landscapes, he would select a focal point in a view, building something there to direct and catch the eye and bring it to rest. In this way, uniformity was broken, and distinction added to the landscape.

> *"When a wide heath, a dreary moor, or a continued plain is in prospect,*
> *objects which catch the eye supply the want of variety; none are so*
> *effectual for this purpose as buildings".*
> Whately's *Observations on Modern Gardening*, 1770

Once set along the long drive to Wroxton from Banbury, and originally called the Castle, this eyecatcher was designed to be a *'notable object'*, and so it is, even though it is now away across fields instead of the park with a view back to the obelisk.

Trees have grown up concealing the eyecatcher from the Abbey from which it was once visible, but like all Miller's work it is equally enjoyable close to. This was his country: his estate at Radway is only a few miles away, and he knew the land and its stone. This Castle is a simple, symmetrical folly, a large central stepped arch flanked by two slender half-round towers, but its stone, a rich, warm sandstone, and its situation, make it memorable - though the approach view from Banbury was not considered at all.

Miller did other work at Wroxton Abbey, producing the now-demolished Gothick temple and also a new tower for the fourteenth-century church. We must never forget that Miller was an amateur architect. When Horace Walpole visited, he commented:

Dovecote

...the tower is in good plain Gothic style, and was once, so they tell you, still more beautiful, but Mr. Miller, who designed it, unluckily once in his life, happened to think rather of beauty than of water-tables, and so it fell down the first winter.

The Castle

ROUSHAM

Sanderson Miller designed the eyecatcher at Wroxton, but it was his great predecessor, Willam Kent, who produced the Oxfordshire Cotswolds' other notable example. In 1738, Kent was called in by General Sir James Dormer to apply his vision of the 'picturesque' to Rousham House. Starting immediately, he remodelled the house and landscaped the relatively small garden nestling in a bend in the river Cherwell to such effect that it became a blueprint for succeeding landscape architects and is generally regarded as his masterpiece.

The making of the garden was a landmark in the history of the Romantic movement, one of the earliest embodiments of the idea of the 'Picturesque', which was not fully expressed as a respectable theory of aesthetics until the last decade of the eighteenth century. The notion of the naturalistic landscape had first become fashionable in literary circles and James Dormer was a friend of Pope, Gay and Swift. A second major influence was the painting of the irregular beauty of the 'Roman' countryside by the Poussin brothers, with nostalgic references to classical antiquity and the bucolic poetry of Virgil. Kent was an unsuccessful painter who had spent ten years in Italy and knew their work. The two came together, here.

The gardens at Rousham are all serpentine curves, and certainly reflect those fashionable theories of the *'line of beauty'* which had become a joke by the time they were published in Hogarth's *'Analysis of Beauty'* of 1753: they were the first reaction to geometric layout in an attempt to make a naturalistic layout. Also, in these early stages evocative *'objects in the landscape'* seem more important than naturalism. In the second half of the eighteenth century the passion for nostalgic ruins and temples subsided, and a milder form of landscape became fashionable in the work of 'Capability' Brown. Rousham represents therefore the first phase of English landscape design and remains almost as Kent left it.

In 1712 Addison, in the *Spectator,* criticised the formal garden with its straight vistas and clipped trees with the remark that *'... a man might make a pretty landskip of his whole possessions'.* Kent's genius lay in opening up such vistas outside the garden to involve the surrounding landscape. He was also aware of the need to demonstrate the element of surprise required in 'Picturesque' composition - following Pope's advice on planning a garden:

> *Let not each beauty everywhere be spied.*
> *When half the skill is decently to hide*
> *He gains all points who pleasingly confounds*
> *Surprises, varies and conceals the bounds.*

Aware that a view needed to be answered, Kent erected two structures to catch the eye. One involved the transformation of an old mill into *'The Temple of the Mill',* a working mill *'rusticated'* into Gothick by Kent to form an *'object',* complete with flying buttresses, stepped gables and a quatrefoil window and which was given more pinnacles and 'improved' considerably, although it has now lost its top.

The other is very different, a straightforward eyecatcher, the first ever built, in about 1740, really a screen standing on a hill a mile to the north of the House. The large tripartite arch is perfectly flat, only relieved with supporting buttresses, and pierced with three openings; blank side wings support the curved top along which stand little pinnacles like the teeth of a sawfish. It is a very plain folly but a very economical one. Close to, the basic structure is seen to be severely rectangular, the curved top seeming to be a later infill; there is no record to show if this was Kent's original intention, although it is clear that the eyecatcher was intended to be a triumphal arch celebrating General Dormer's victories in Spain.

Eyecatcher, Rousham

The garden itself had temples, cascades, grottos, terraces and statues added. One of the most satisfactory ornaments - it is certainly no folly in this climate - is the *Praeneste,* an elegant covered arcade of six beautiful bold arches in which to stroll in the rain, for which Kent designed the seats and which he flanked with superb urns.

Visitors were enthusiastic about the garden, described by Horace Walpole as *'Daphne in little'.* Those who were not guests at the House entered through a Palladian Gateway designed by Kent on the public road, and flanked by niches with statues and preceded by urns. Beside it is a castellated Lodge with classical arches, one half of which is a cow-house, the other a sheltered seat - truly a curious manifestation of the interest in the decorative farmstead or *ferme ornee!*

Praeneste, Rousham

Farms were favourite subjects for treatment by folly-builders and three other country houses in Oxfordshire display eyecatchers.

CHARLBURY

Location Seven miles south of Chipping Norton, south of A44. Sheet 164 39092121

Ditchley Park was laid out by James Gibbs in the 1720s and remodelled by 'Capability' Brown in 1770. Here William Kent worked inside the house rather than in the garden, although Lodge Farm, built as an eyecatcher to the south, has an elaborate design with some qualities of his strained Gothick. The facade facing the House has three projecting arches in the centre, formerly open but now filled with a door and windows. Gothick traceried windows illuminate the side wings and five quatrefoil windows the first floor. The quatrefoils and arches are repeated in woodwork superimposed on a wall of a barn to the west, which from afar would look like windows but are in fact blind. At the rear, the windows are all Gothic but the facade is plain. The farm cannot be seen from Ditchley House itself, but stands out clearly from the Ditchley-Blenheim road.

In the Park itself are two temples: one Tuscan, originally by the lake but moved nearer the house in 1930, and the other a round Ionic temple, most probably built by Stiff Leadbetter in 1760 but which has been attributed also to Henry Holland. At the head of the lake is a three-arched stone grotto.

COLESHILL

Strattenborough Castle farm near Coleshill, has a splendid sham facade, dated 1792, on the back of an otherwise unremarkable farmhouse, and was built both as an eyecatcher from Coleshill House and to hide the working farm buildings.

The facade is constructed partly in stone and partly in brick. The stone follows the outline of a ruined medieval castle, and brick is used to complete the house. The stone front is charming, with its mock windows, turrets and battlements, but the most convincing part is the brick infill, without which the western wall of the front would crumble away to ruin.

The two main walls are high and level with it; the remains of the battlements can be seen on the top. At one side is a barn with stepped gables, and incorporated in a barn wall on the other side are the sham remains of a massive round-arched window, looking like a ruined chapel, with underneath and set into the wall the carved figure of a man on a horse, giving the appearance of early medieval.

Coleshill Hill Park lies a mile away across the valley. From the house which stood there until 1952, Strattenborough Castle must have appeared exactly as the designer had visualised - a vanquished rival in picturesque decay.

COKETHORPE

Location Two miles south of Witney, on the A415. Sheet 164 37420661

The quaintly named Fish House Mill at Cokethorpe also received the eyecatcher facade treatment, this time to make a viewpoint from Cokethorpe Park.

Attached to a cottage which was itself left untouched, the square mill-house was battlemented and ornamented with heavily crocketed pinnacles both in the centre and at the corners of each wall, and given Tudor windows. It stands three storeys high and carries a datestone of 1723, which is clearly too early for this sort of treatment. It is more likely to have been modified later in the eighteenth century when that form of activity was in vogue: in support of this dating, the tower includes masonry taken from Stanton Harcourt manor, which was not demolished until about 1750.

GREAT BARRINGTON

Location Three miles west of Burford, north of A40. Sheet 163 20531350

In 1735, after the Bray family had owned the manor of Great Barrington almost from the dissolution of Llanthony Priory two hundred years previously, Reginald Bray sold the estate to Lord Chancellor Talbot, who intended it as a home for his son, William. The money for the purchase came from Lord Talbot's wife, Mary de Cardonell, whose father had a post in the Government which he had exploited to the full. Only a year later, the old house was badly damaged by fire and it was decided to build a new one on a natural terrace overlooking the river Windrush. Plans were approved and work may even have started before Lord Talbot's early death in 1737, after which his brother paid the bills presented by the builder, William Smith of Warwick. Whether Smith was also the designer or whether it was William Kent, as has been suggested, is intriguing, for no documentary proof exists either way. The Palladian mansion, referred to by Pope in his *Use of Riches, 'At Barrington shall English Bounty stand'*, was finished in 1738.

Garden temples entered the English scene early in the eighteenth century, transferred, especially into the landscapes pioneered by William Kent, from the paintings of Poussin and Claude Lorraine. These 'Grecian' temples reminded those who strolled in the landscape gardens, or entered the temple's shade and coolness, of all the graces and virtues - temples of such deities as Venus and Diana, of Ancient Virtue or of Friendship. Away from the country house, in the wider landscape, the Gothic ruin might agree with the genius of the native scene; nearer the house, in the contemplative garden, beauty and wholeness and dignity were appropriate in emblems of polite culture - temples. But before long champions of the natural began to disapprove; by the turn of the century temples of all kinds were under attack by connoisseurs.

In the mid-eighteenth century, William Talbot was created Earl Talbot and at this time the Park was landscaped. The river Windrush was diverted to form an ornamental water, and a number of buildings were erected to embellish the Park. These included a Gothick Temple with ogee arches, a Pigeon House with a dome (the lead cupola was removed in 1920) and an Ionic tetrastyle portico, and a circular Roman Doric temple in the garden. Stylistically this circular garden temple and the Pigeon House have been attributed to William Kent but even though in practice none of the buildings may have been by him they are of considerable inventiveness.

Roman Temple, Barrington Hall

BARNSLEY

Location Five miles north-west of Cirencester, on the B4425. Sheet 163 08120580

The road from Cirencester to Bibury passes through Barnsley, where it obeys the dictates of a low wall behind which ancient trees whet the appetite but do not afford the glimpse of the house - one of the most unusual and exciting in the Cotswolds, certainly the best example of an eighteenth-century, uncompromisingly Baroque country house, of national importance. And yet the almost complete absence of documentation has made the identity of its designer - or designers - a matter of continuing speculation; ingeniously planned, superbly built, and lavishly decorated, it has not been attributed with any certainty to any particular architect.

The background to the building of the house is reasonably clear. In 1700, Brereton Bourchier of Barnsley House married Catherine Brydges, daughter of the 8th Lord Chandos. Catherine was not a wealthy heiress, but between 1705 and 1713 her brother, James, amassed a fortune as Paymaster of the Forces under the Duke of Marlborough, and went on to become the Duke of Chandos. Bourchier died in 1713, leaving debts and an only daughter, Martha, aged ten, by a second marriage. She inherited the Barnsley estate, although Bourchier's widow acted as a trustee during her daughter's minority. In 1719, while still a minor, Martha married Henry Perrot of North Leigh in Oxfordshire, who was 30, a hanger-on member of her uncle's circle, something of a dilettante, and later MP for Oxfordshire.

That Mrs Bouchier had been sister to a nobleman of immense riches and an obsession for building may help explain Brereton Bourchier's itch to build at Barnsley where his forebears had settled since Henry VIII's reign. But who designed Barnsley Park? The main responsibility was probably that of John James, perhaps with the advice or subject to approval of Nicholas Hawksmoor, who had collaborated with Vanbrugh in the building of Blenheim.

The house was finally completed in 1731. Mrs Perrot died the following year, predeceasing her husband Henry, who died in Paris in 1740. On his death two spinster daughters, Martha (d.1773) and Cassandra (d.1778) reigned at Barnsley Park. In 1778, Cassandra left the estate to a distant relation, James Musgrave, a young man of twenty-seven and a descendant of her father's sister. He eventually succeeded to a baronetcy and was responsible for the later decorative styles introduced to the house. It was he who first employed John Nash between 1806 and 1813.

In grand gardens, a tiled-roofed 'greenshouse' was used to protect evergreens during the winter, for glass-roofing and proper heating did not appear until the nineteenth century. In many instances, this evolved into the conservatory, like the greenhouse a glass-covered structure for tender plants but unlike it usually accessible from the house and highly decorative. Orange and lemon trees were the first tender evergreens to adorn British gardens. In winter they had to be protected from the vagaries of the British climate so were housed in an Orangery, which in design developed into the most ornate of the early plant houses. Here is a splendid example of such a garden building, a detached Orangery composed of a serried row of Ionic columns between glazed openings and end pediments of pretty glass roundels, designed by John Nash and built between 1807 and 1810.

Innovatively, Nash brought the 'new' structural material of cast iron into the roof support - probably the first time it had been employed in this way. A series of descending circular iron hoops both support the glazed roof and enable the air-vent lights to be opened, a design echoed in the wood tracery of the windows on both gable pediments. Amazingly, the builder-mason charged only £12 for his work - even accepting that he would live on the premises and that the stone would come from local quarries, this seems remarkably good value for the team of stone-workers who turned the columns, carved the capitals, built the base and erected the structure, a project which must have taken the equivalent of at least eighteen months labour.

Another little building designed by this Regency architect is the Bibury Lodge, an octagonal lodge with a small segmental covered arcade leading to the gate, and often known as the Pepper Pot.

Barnsley House, on the other side of the road, is actually older than the Park, with a date stone of 1697. It was built for the same Bourchier family, and was the rectory from 1762 to 1932. This has two delightful garden buildings, an elegant Gothick alcove of c.1770 in its original position facing north, and a Tuscan Doric Temple built originally c.1787 but moved here from Fairford Park in 1962.

CIRENCESTER

Location At the junction of A429, A417 and A419. Sheet 163 97390319

In 1695, Sir Benjamin Bathurst, a member of an ancient and wealthy family from Sussex, purchased the western Tything of Oakley. He was the youngest of thirteen brothers, six of whom had lost their lives fighting for King Charles I in the Civil Wars, and had become a Governor of the East India Company. Through his marriage to a daughter of Sir Allen Apsley, a royalist in high favour at Court, Sir Benjamin was made Falconer to King Charles II, became Treasurer of the Household of Princess Anne, and on her accession to the throne, her Cofferer. He died in 1704, having already made over the Cirencester property to his eldest son, Allen.

Allen Bathurst was a young man of twenty who at the age of eight had been contracted, *'in jest to please his grandmother'*, to marry his first cousin, Catherine Apsley, then aged four. On the death of Sir Benjamin, the marriage was re-enacted and for seventy-six years the couple remained man and wife. Even before he came of age, Allen was elected MP for Cirencester. Politically ambitious, he rapidly made his way in parliamentary circles and in 1712 was one of a dozen Tories raised to the peerage to swamp the Upper House and induce the Lords to endorse the Treaty of Utrecht. On Queen Anne's death in 1714 the Tories were discredited and Baron Bathurst, later the 1st Earl, found himself faced with unexpected early retirement from active politics.

He did not mind in the least. He was delighted to live the greater part of the year in the country and began to show very considerable talents in other directions. He turned his attention to the improvement first of his house, and then of his estate, to create a park incorporating the latest notions of taste and fashion. To begin with the existing handsome Jacobean house, Oakley Grove, was demolished and rebuilt between 1714 and 1718, for which he was almost certainly his own architect and which was in many respects as conservative and unassertive as his politics. Bathurst's decision to use the foundations of the earlier house rather than to rebuild it on a new site away from the town, as was the Whig custom, ensured that it remained an adjunct of the town and not become aloof and isolated in its park, which was in keeping with his Tory sympathies. He merely distanced his new property from the town by a three-quarter circle of high yew hedge in the manner of Bernini's colonnade before St. Peter's, but on an infinitely smaller scale. Bathurst appears to have been fairly indifferent to the appearance of his country seat, remarking airily to his cousin, Lord Strafford:

I think any house good enough to sleep in,

and wrote, when the work was finished, to the poet and fellow-Tory, Alexander Pope, of whom he was friend and patron,

I trust you to give an account how it comes to be so oddly bad.

Bathurst's indifference to building did not continue for long. By 1718, he was in correspondence with Pope in the latter's capacity as a leading figure in London gardening circles. Pope is as easily appreciated now as a garden designer and grand-master of style as he is a poet. He would have seen all three roles as expressions of Classicism, the ordered, elegant style of the Augustan Age. His output of all three was colossal in spite of crippling ill-health from childhood that left him less then five feet tall with a spinal deformity and in spite of spending so much time dining and quarrelling with fellow-writers in London, or lodging with literary-minded lords in their stately homes.

Pope was ever ready to help *'dear Bathurst'*. Together, they planned his life's work, namely the creation of the 3,000 acre parkscape, designing woods, walks and neo-Classical follies, and determining to

> *... open avenues, cut glades, plant firs, contrive water-works all very fine and beautiful ...*

In 1716, Bathurst had bought the Oakley estate, west of Cirencester, from the executors of Sir Robert Atkyns, whom he despised, and whose splendid Jacobean house, like Oakley Grove, he demolished. Alexander Pope's classical learning and vision and the Earl's taste and practical experience as an horticulturist now combined to produce the largest area of early Georgian landscape layout to survive in Britain. Pope invested some of his own capital in the enterprise, the Earl promising him

> *... three or four million plants out of my own nursery to amuse yourself with ...*

and later Pope wrote of how he and his patron would

> *... draw plans for houses and gardens ... all very fine and beautiful in our imagination.*

Pope's influence is everywhere. He helped Bathurst plan and develop the Park with a proprietorial enthusiasm, even going as far as to call it *'my bower'*, and recording his involvement in the couplet

> *Who then shall grace or who improve the soil,*
> *Who plants like Bathurst or who builds like Boyle.*

Their conception developed slowly, and became more informal as it developed, but the bones of the layout remained great rides cut through woodland, much of which Bathurst was responsible for planting. The area between Cirencester and Sapperton they proceeded to lay out as a series of parks united by one immensely long avenue seventy-five yards wide and not closely defined by planting particular trees (as for example at Badminton), thus giving the impression of being cut through natural woods; nor was it centred on the house but runs from the Lodge gates through Oakley Wood. In this way Lord Bathurst achieved a wonderful balance between the formality of the grand avenue and the picturesque eighteenth-century garden. Consequently, the Park stretches from the middle of the town for five miles into the countryside, and the mansion itself acts both as the straight arc of the huge yew-circle hedge, a device repeated by the Ten Rides *rond-point* in Oakley Wood, and as the view-point for a 'prospect' centred on Kemble church. Chestnut, elm and oak trees were used to give variety to the dominant beech, and yews and other conifers were introduced where a sombre atmosphere was desired. Bathurst laid great emphasis on seasonal colouring, and his calculated efforts to achieve it contribute to his reputation as a great gardener.

The famous beech plantations attract foresters from all over the world, and we can marvel at the scale of Pope's recommendations:

> *Join Cotswold Hills to Sapperton's fair dale ...*
> *Link towns to towns with avenues of oak,*
> *Enclose whole downs in walls, 'tis all a joke!*
> *Inexorable Death shall level all,*
> *And trees, and stones, and farms, and farmer fall.*

Pope was devoted to the young, handsome, genial lord:

> *Oh teach us Bathurst Yet unspoiled by wealth!*
> *That secret rare, between the extremes to move*
> *Of mad good nature, and of mean self-love*

declaimed Epistle III of the *Moral Essays,* dedicated to the Earl. Bathurst returned Pope's affection and bore his reproaches ('Batty' was an unpredictable, impetuous, unpunctual gadabout, not to be depended upon) with wry amusement. Though they were the closest of collaborators, Pope was not the only member of the literati whom Bathurst befriended: Congreve, Prior, Gay, Atterbury and Sterne were either correspondents or visitors or both, and to whose advice he listened. During his visit in 1726, Pope was accompanied by friend and fellow-satirist Jonathan Swift, carrying with him the manuscript of *Gulliver's Travels.*

A certain respect for natural features was ever in the Earl's mind. Pope had advised that

> *... there is something in the amiable Simplicity of unadorn'd Nature ...*

and where Bathurst found irregularly shaped woods and glades they were kept that way. An artificial lake, again irregular in shape and made to look as natural as possible, a complete departure from the formal canal and an early example of the new fashion, and an occasional serpentine walk add a note of studied picturesqueness.

As well as creating noble plantations of trees and laying out avenues, a host of decorative buildings slowly appeared as Bathurst littered his landscape with temples and follies - including the very first *'romantick'* seen in England. The form of these may have been suggested by Pope but for the most part Bathurst designed them himself. He became an early proponent of the Gothick Revival and it is for this that his garden buildings are chiefly remarkable.

The siting of the buildings may look random, but was undertaken with great care. Past the Lodge gates, the Broad Avenue rises slightly and about two hundred yards on the right, set back in a clearing, is the Hexagon, exactly what its name says: three open and three blind arches, set on a plinth. Built in 1736, it is a temple of massive order, chamfered heavy rustication from plinth to impost blocks, keystones and voussoirs, though now the Cotswold stone is beautifully lichened purple and yellow. Architecturally it is not very exciting, and similar buildings can be seen in every eighteenth-century pattern book, but in winter, thinly seen through the mist, and with brown leaves and the yellow earth, it is very pleasing. Clearly it is a building which adapts perfectly to every seasonal change of light and colour.

The Avenue continues up the hill to the crest. Here on the right, amongst the trees, is a small, vermiculated rusticated stone Doric temple flanked by niches, inscribed *'Pope's Seat'*, facing south across Seven Rides *rond-point* down the avenue centred on Kemble church. It is an elegant but again unremarkable Classical composition such as many gentlemen built in their parks in the 1720s and 1730s.

The Hexagon

Pope's Seat

The trees are thinner here, and the broad ride continues past the Horse Guards, two ornamental arches with Ionic pilasters, moulded abaci, frieze, paterae, and dentil cornice, the arches having plain ashlar dressings with impost blocks and keystones. They are really a pair of gargantuan sentry boxes which stand on either side of the Avenue to the Round House, at Ten Rides *rond-point*. The Round House is a round tower, with the usual slits and castellations, joined to a low brick cottage. The ride then goes on through the trees, emerging suddenly into open ground where the main avenue becomes a wide grassy space surrounding the crenellated Square Tower. This is a little square cottage, the walls rising in castellations in front, and at the west end is a small square tower which just rises above the level of the main roof.

Round House

Square Tower

The drive continues across the open park to Ivy Lodge, a delicious fantasy, half-farmhouse and half-farm buildings, with castellations and Gothic windows. In the centre of a long facade of yellow Cotswold stone is a square tower, and at either end is a crow-stepped gable. The right-hand tower and the gable have mullioned windows with leaded glass, and hide a splendid barn. The left-hand gable also has mullioned windows, but the lead for the glass is scored on the cement infill, for this end of the building is merely a screen-wall wind-break protecting an orchard behind.

Ivy Lodge

At the centre of Oakley Wood, the furthest point of the park from the house, Bathurst built a lodge of hewn stone. Called successively The Hermitage in the Wood, King Arthur's Castle and finally King Alfred's Hall, this folly was begun in 1721 and completed eleven years later after reams of correspondence with Atterbury, Swift and Pope as to its progress and ultimate style. It is the ancestor of all castellated Gothic follies in Georgian parkscapes and was started twenty years before Sanderson Miller's tower on Edgehill - it is worth noting that Pope had already started the first grotto, at his house at Twickenham. The original appearance of the lodge is unknown: it may have been quite small, no more than a tentative essay, but about 1730 Bathurst demolished Sapperton Manor and took windows, doorways, battlements and sculpture from the Jacobean house to give the Hall a Gothick appearance, and enlarged it in 1732.

Gothic window, King Alfred's Hall

Alfred's Hall is a true sham, the best as well as the first. In an age of symmetry Bathurst abandoned all regularity and created

> *the real horrid feeling of conglomeration,*

a feature emphasised by the choice of location, here made forbidding by evergreens, yew and fir, so that light is filtered through a green gloom onto the 'ruin'. Rhododendrons and laurels crowd up to the mouldering walls, and the clearing of grass in front of the building is bordered with black trees.

Basically, Alfred's Hall is a long room screened on all sides with castellated walls, the main front facing the clearing. To the right of the two entrance doors the wall comes forward in a semi-circle, turns back in a wall pierced with a Gothick window, and then fades down to the ground. To the left, the curtain walls are more elaborate, pierced with broken doorways and windows and interrupted with small buttresses. Behind this wall is a small courtyard with steps down to a cellar and up to a room above; the interior is wainscoted, with a large carved chimneypiece. Here too is the shell of a semi-circular tower. From the back, Alfred's Hall could not be mistaken for a ruin as here it is a real structure, but there are some odd stained-glass windows.

So successful and unexpected was the unique asymmetric design of Bathurst's construction that a visitor soon afterwards took it for the remains of the old family home

> *...built with stone, in the old manner, with battlements round the top, and*
> *a tower with an old gate to go into it, which gives it much the look of a*
> *Castle; this my Lord has left a good deal of standing, and furnish'd it,*
> *and makes a summer house of it, and it is a very Romantick pretty place.*

It was admired immensely by the Earl's friends and visitors, the diarist Mrs Delaney declaring that the twelve-year-old building had been mistaken by one learned archaeologist as undoubtedly a residence of King Arthur.

Bathurst and Pope made of Alfred's Hall a building which it is difficult to equal as a convincing sham, achieving the amorphous squalor of the Middle Ages: eighteenth-century neatness is seen only in the lettering of *Alfred's Hall* over the main entrance. It was used for *al fresco* meals on summer evenings, and was also the scene of an annual music meeting where the country folk assembled to pass the time in fiddling, dancing and drinking.

Draped in ivy and enclosed by a grove of melancholy yews, its setting is still romantic. Sadly, Alfred's Hall is now alarmingly delapidated and part of it has recently collapsed: this sham ruin which has lasted for over 270 years is in danger of becoming a real one, though there are plans for its restoration. Despite this, it was carefully made, unlike many of its imitators; Bathurst was determined his buildings would last and virtually every embellishment he made to the Park survives.

When Bathurst began to plant he was thirty years old: he lived another sixty years, almost but not quite to complete his work. Indeed, the Park has remained unaltered primarily because the 1st Earl lived to such a considerable age and did not succumb to changes in fashion which followed quickly on his landscaping projects. It was though left to his son, the 2nd Earl who became Lord Chancellor, to extend Broad Avenue to its full five-mile limit, focussed oddly enough on Cirencester church tower. To within a month of his death at the age of ninety-one, Bathurst rode two hours a day and drank, without fail, a bottle of claret or madeira after dinner. The straight-laced Lord Chancellor disapproved of this harmless addiction but the man who once said that the four most desirable things in life were

old wood to burn, old wine to drink, old friends to converse with, and old books to read,

paid him no heed whatever. On the contrary, one of the last glimpses we get of the Earl comes through a dinner guest at Cirencester when his host was already a nonagenarian: the meal over, the abstemious son withdrew from the table, whereupon the father cried jubilantly,

Come, now the old gentleman's gone, let us crack another bottle!

When Lord Bathurst finally died in 1775 the Park was unfinished but it has matured under the caring hands of successive Earls Bathurst, so that it remains, as it has been since the early eighteenth century, the finest woodland landscape in England.

The folly-building notion was taken up again later by others. Just outside the Lodge gates, in Cecily Hill, stand the Barracks, built in the late nineteenth century as a folly castle, and never used to house soldiers.

The Barracks

48

SIDDINGTON

Location One mile south of Cirencester, east of A419.   Sheet 163   04299964

A local landmark is a charming little three-storey tapering round tower, castellated, and accompanied by a lone pine tree.

It probably dates from the late eighteenth century but its origination is indeterminate. On a map of 1824, it is identified as a windmill, and a lease exists referring to a wind grist mill in Siddington built by the Earl Bathurst: it is of course possible that when the sails were removed, the battlements were added. On the other hand, local tradition maintains that in spite of its appearance it never was a windmill but was built, along with two cottages nearby, by a Dutchman who settled in the district and reminded him nostalgically of his homeland. Whether it is either a castellated folly or a modified windmill, it resembles very closely a chess rook.

FARINGDON

Even in the conformist twentieth century, the tradition of eccenticity has been upheld. Lord Berners' Folly, as it was known from the start, is the last major folly tower to have been built. For several years the plans for its erection had been attended by a frenzy of strenuous protest and conflict in this market town: the 14th Lord Berners faced an issue that never troubled the original folly builders. Eventually the decision of the local council to withhold planning consent was over-ridden by higher powers from the Ministry. During the summer months of 1935, a fantastic tower started to take shape on the crest of a wooded hillock, the site of a medieval castle and a Cromwellian battery. Amongst wild rumours and the furious complaints of the local gentry, the tower grew higher until by the end of the year it was completed. It rose to a height of one hundred and forty feet, and was topped by a great octagonal lantern, from which, after scrambling up a narrow spiral stair, one could gaze for miles across the fields of several counties, to the Berkshire Downs and to the White Horse of Uffington.

Gerald Tyrwhitt-Wilson, 14th Lord Berners, was unmoved by the storm. Artist, author, musician of sparkling talent, retired honorary diplomat who was inclined to practical jokes, and who had dreamed up, organised and financed the whole project from his Palladian villa on the edge of the market town, where doves dyed to every shade of the rainbow fluttered over sloping lawns, and birds of paradise and whippets with diamond collars wandered amongst a priceless collection of treasures, declared with his usual understated flippancy:

> *The great point of the tower is that it will be entirely useless.*
> *I want to stand on top of it and look around me.*

That was not quite the case, for it was built during the 1930s depression and provided valuable work for the unemployed - so it was not as useless as his Lordship made out. He had inherited his title in 1918 - he later held that this was only because three of his uncles fell off a bridge at the same time. In fact, he came into two titles, one of which dated back to the fifteenth century, three houses and a large fortune. In his entry in *Who's Who,* Lord Berners listed his recreations as *'none',* but this was only another instance of his flippancy. When not writing, painting or composing - he was the only English composer to be directly commissioned by Diaghilev - he was establishing a ranch in Spain to breed fighting bulls or training a pack of hounds to forage for truffles on the Berkshire woods or surprising his guests by reading the newspaper upside down. He remained a bachelor all his life, but listed six requirements for a happy marriage:

> *A short memory*
> *A long purse*
> *Infinite incredulity*
> *A combative nature*
> *The man should be a man, and the*
> *Woman a woman, or vice versa.*

The tower was actually designed by Trenwith Wills and Lord Gerald Wellesley, later the 7th Duke of Wellington, and the culmination of its construction was a grand party and splendid firework display on the fifth of November with the release of hundreds of doves dyed in pastel shades of red, white and blue.

It is plain rather than ugly. Originally, it was colour-washed cream, but no trace of this remains. Now gaunt ribbed bricks rear up 120 feet with a tiny wood-framed window, devoid of ornament, on each side. At the top is a small square belvedere room with three arched windows on each side On the top, an octagonal pinnacled room, with elongated oblong windows, stands as the only decoration. Although it is only just over sixty years old it already appears ruinous: the mortar has fallen from between the bricks, the glass has gone, and the entrance had to be blocked up twenty years ago. Inside is a rotting wooden staircase, but for those brave or foolhardy enough to risk life and limb by getting to the top, the view on a clear day was a sight to behold.

Just as the erection of the Tower provided a source of income at a time of great need for many local people, Lord Berner also thought that there could be someone who might find it a useful means of leaving the problems of this world behind. So he left a neat notice, which read: *Members of the public committing suicide from this tower do so at their own risk.*

When he died in 1950, his friends mourned an unforgettable person, a creative artist, wit and humorist, and a fantasy world he had constructed. He wrote his own epitaph:

Here lies Lord Berners
One of the learners.
His great love of learning
May earn him a burning.
But praise the Lord
He never was bored!

Interestingly, the first building to greet the visitor to Faringdon is a pub called *The Folly,* but which has nothing to do with the Tower and has had its name since long before 1935. The clump of trees (feuillee) on the hill was planted in the eighteenth century by Henry Pye, then the Poet Laureate, who wrote a poem, *Faringdon Hill,* about the site which has been known as Faringdon Folly for at least 200 years. So Lord Berners may have been the last folly tower builder, but he had maintained the local tradition immaculately.

MIDDLE LYPIATT

Location Two miles west of Stroud, north of A419. Sheet 162 88500548

The origin of Lypiatt Park was secular, not monastic. It stands on the site of the manor of Over Lypiatt, where a house with gardens was recorded as long ago as 1324. At this time the property belonged to the Maunsell family, and it remained in their ownership until 1395 when Richard Whittington, the celebrated three-times Mayor of London, obtained it in satisfaction of a debt. In 1610 Lypiatt was bought from the descendants of a Robert Wye by Thomas Stephens, but although he and his family lived here and were prominent local men, nothing was done to alter and enlarge their old-fashioned house. On January 1, 1645, Lypiatt was captured and burnt by Royalist troops evicting a Parliamentary garrison, but even then the house was repaired, not rebuilt. Any dramatic reshaping of the building had to wait. In 1800, when Thomas Baghot-de-la-Bere of Southam, nephew of the last Stephens owner, offered for sale

> *...the capital mansion house called Lypiat-House, with the Courts,*
> *Yards, Gardens, Park and Pleasure Grounds,*

it was still the unspoilt sixteenth-century manor house. It was bought in 1802 by Paul Wathen of Woodchester, a clothier-cum-banker who sought to cement his success and social respectability by the purchase of a landed estate. That year was also one of great distress for the cloth workers, who were prompted to write about the new shearing machines to Wathen, a man arrogant with wealth and his new position as one of the landed gentry:

> *Wee Here in Form you get Sheer in mee sheens and if you dont pull them down in a*
> *fortnights time Wee will pull them down for you, Damned infernal Dog. And before*
> *Almighty God we will pull down all your mills that have Meany Sheer in me Sheens in.*
> *We will cut out your Damned Hearts and will make the rest Heat them.*

How clearly is illustrated the change in the paternal attitude to employees of the early days of the trade when the mill-owner lived near his mill and his work-people.

Paul Wathen was a friend of the Prince Regent. In 1810 he served as High Sheriff of the county, an expensive office traditionally filled by such social aspirants, and in 1812 he was knighted by the Prince so that he might stand proxy for Lord Strangford, the British ambassador in Lisbon, at a ceremony in which the the Order of the Bath was conferred on Strangford; he also changed his name from Wathen to the more historic Baghott. At the same time as all this social climbing was in progress, Wathen began alterations to Lypiatt Park. The architect selected was Jeffrey Wyatt, who changed his name to Wyatville some years later and perhaps shared some of Baghott's romantic fantasies of wealth and lineage. Wyatt began by producing schemes for rebuilding Lypiatt on a suitably grand scale as a picturesque castle, one of which was exhibited at the Royal Academy in 1809, when it was said to be *'now building'*.

It soon became clear, however, that Baghott's finances were not sufficiently robust to withstand the cyclical nature of business activity, and during the second decade of the century his affairs became increasingly desperate. He was also squandering the fortune that his father, a local clothier, had made by consorting with the Prince and his companions, indulging in all the extravagances of the period. Knowing of this recklessness it is little wonder the workmen sent a threatening letter, though it had no effect on his way of life.

The plans for Lypiatt were eventually scaled down to a remodelling of the old house and the addition of a new wing, and the work was well-advanced though unfinished when Baghott finally went bankrupt in 1819. Amongst other modifications, an embattled three-storey tower was added to the west end of the hall block, and to connect this with the surviving medieval chapel a Gothic cloister was built. Although it has since been extended and altered, Wyatville's work still forms the central and most impressive part of the house.

Wyatville and Baghott worked not only on the house, but on its environs as well. Sale particulars in 1846 refer to the house with routine hyperbole as

> ...the most elegant and complete Chateau that can be found
> among England's boasted beauties,

but the *'ivy-mantled Towers and Walls'* of the stables, coach-houses and lodge contribute much of the undeniably romantic air of the estate, and must have accounted for a significant proportion of Baghott's considerable expenditure. Some of these buildings may, however, have been due to Baghott's successor, William Lewis of Brimscombe, who bought the estate in about 1824, since the lodge fronts onto a turnpike road created only in 1823. Lewis was himself a clothier, and suffered financial difficulties in the depression which affected the Gloucestershire cloth industry from 1826 onwards. He retained Lypiatt, however, until 1842, when it was sold to Samuel Baker, who began further alterations soon afterwards.

NETHER LYPIATT

The manor house - though strictly speaking it never has been a manor house - stands high on an escarpment looking west over Stroud and east over Toadsmoor Bottom. When one is least expecting, it suddenly appears set back from a lane, behind a screen of stone piers linked by iron grilles. Harold Nicholson wrote in his diary in 1947, on a visit with his wife:

I am entranced by the house which is the only
one which we have seen that I really covet.

Nether Lypiatt is not most people's idea of a typical Cotswold house. Though it has been called 'a minor masterpiece', it is rather un-English, a compact tall building looking backwards to a style of half a century before, to the form of a post-Reformation hunting lodge. In beautiful mauve-coloured stone, it is an exact cube, forty-five feet square, and on all four fronts symmetry is strictly observed. The stone-tiled roof sweeps over coved eaves and the tall panelled chimney stacks give a vertical emphasis that is the perfect counterpoise to the horizontal rhythm of the fenestration.

The Freame family had a house close to the present exposed site by 1509. At the death of Thomas Freame in 1689 the estate was divided between co-heiresses, one of whom Anne Chamberlayne, obtained the house. Her daughter, Catherine, and her husband Charles Coxe, inherited the property in 1699, and also acquired some of the land from one of Catherine's aunts. The present house was built by this Charles Coxe. However, the architect is not known and there is even some confusion about the precise date of its construction.

Charles Coxe held the property until his death in 1728. By profession he was a Judge, and held various legal posts of distinction: Justice of the Brecon, Radnor and Glamorganshire Circuit, and Judge Clerk of the Patent Office among them; he was also MP for Cirencester and later for Gloucester. However, this distinguished man has been resolved into an arch-villain. He is said to have reprieved an iron-smith from the death sentence on condition that he fashioned the beautiful gates and screen in front of the house; and that because the smith did not make them strictly symmetrical Coxe retracted as soon as the work was finished and the smith was duly hanged - but not until after cursing the Judge and his house. There is nothing but legend to support the charge, nevertheless in the three centuries following it the manor has never passed from father to son, as the smith swore it should never do. There is though visible proof of a tender side to the Judge's character, in the monumental obelisk which he raised to his horse in a dell to the south of the house.

The Greeks gave four-sided Egyptian pillars capped with a pyramidion the name *obeliskus,* a little spit. The pharaohs had set them up in front of temples, where they belonged to the sun god, as a formalisation of rough standing stones; the pyramidion on top was covered with copper and caught the first and last rays of the sun. Succeeding civilisations thought of them as trophies of pomp and pride: Egyptian specimens were carried off to Rome, and many home-designed ones erected. From paintings, engravings and recollections of travel, they were imitated in turn by English architects and garden designers of the eighteenth century, and set up in gardens or on hills to give a focal point to the landscape, in deference to the classical spirit expressed in the Palladian mansion, or *vice versa.*

Obelisks were raised as memorials more often than not, meant to suggest or induce, like the urn and the garden temple, a melancholic mood of reverie and reflection. William Kent was on one occasion so affected by melancholy while he sat under one *"that he remained all night, as if enchanted, in that spot until released by the morning sun"*. Having outlived eighteenth-century taste to become a standardised type of public memorial, with associations to match, obelisks have lost their magic. Perhaps they should have been capped with copper like their Egyptian prototypes - but eighteenth-century landlords were less mindful of deity and eternity than the pharaohs and more mindful of cash.

On a bronze plaque on the obelisk, Judge Coxe had inscribed:

> *My name is Wag that rolled the green*
> *The oldest horse that ever was seen*
> *My years - they number forty-two -*
> *I served my master just and true.*

This is a reference to the tradition that Wag rolled the lawns without human guidance. It is alleged also that, equipped with panniers, he would descend to Stroud, effect commissions at the shops and, laden, return by himself. He also haunts the place in a not unpleasant way: the clatter of his hooves may be heard on Christmas Eve, and sometimes he is seen galloping soundlessly through the wood. To relieve you from being worried by these pranks it is wise to deposit a coin or two on the base of Wag's obelisk.

PAINSWICK

Location Five miles south of Gloucester, on the B4073. Sheet 162 86621068

One of the most ambitious restorations of a private garden ever undertaken involves the Rococo Garden. The word 'rococo' is derived from *recaille* (rock work) and *cocquille* (shell), an allusion to oddly-shaped rocks, groups of shells and other natural objects featured artistically with scrolls. In garden design the word describes an asymmetric compromise between formality and informality, the regular with the irregular, and the crowding of many small features into a limited area. This garden is unique, the only complete survivor of that short period in the eighteenth century when gardens in this style were fashionable.

The sequence begins in 1735 when Charles Hyett, an attorney in Gloucester, towards the end of his life bought a small estate called the Herrings. With this came a farmhouse which Hyett promptly demolished and replaced by a new villa which he named *Buenos Ayres,* alluding to Painswick's reputation for healthy air. At the end of the century, as the Hyetts' prosperity and influence expanded, this name was dropped in favour of the grander title, Painswick House.

Hyett died in 1738, almost as soon as his new house was completed, and his son, Benjamin, carried on the process of creating a country seat by turning his attention, in the 1740s, to the gardens. Perhaps because of a difference in temperament between father and son, the worthy, comfortable and sober provincial Classicism of the house here gives way to a more light-hearted, sophisticated scheme. The gardens were depicted in a series of views of 1748 by Thomas Robins, the Rococo landscape painter. His pictures show the gardens newly-planted and may have been painted to celebrate their completion, but it has been suggested that he was also involved in their design, if not the actual designer. One painting is of particular interest for there is some doubt that certain parts shown were actually built, and in this sense the view is of a garden perhaps more imagined than real. Further, it is an ectopic picture, the perspective shown of the garden being impossible to achieve from this (or any) position, let alone from the point where Robins himself drew it (he is shown in the left corner of the painting, seated near the Pigeon House).

The gardens lie not in the front of the house, where they would have been exposed to the south-westerly winds, but in the combe behind it. Following a visit in 1757, Bishop Pococke described how *'the garden is on an hanging ground from the house in a vale, and on a rising ground on the other side and at the end; all are cut into walks through wood and adorn'd with water and buildings.'*

Within the Gothick and rustic features are some wonderful garden buildings, the woodland walks giving glimpses of alcoves, temples and pools. The Red House, an entrancing, asymmetrical, mysteriously two-facaded Gothic gazebo or summer house looking down the main vista of a yew alley directed towards a distant pond, was originally pigmented red, and some traces of this can still be seen. A path passing the Doric Seat leads to the Plunge Pool with its adjacent arched spring head; the water here is very cold and it is doubtful if eighteenth-century gentlemen plunged into it very often, though they would undoubtedly have played bowls on the Green nearby. The curious Pigeon House is octagonal outside with eight windows, but circular inside with only four! The Eagle House is an airy Gothick

Exedra

Pigeon House

gazebo or pavilion with pinnacles, crockets and pointed windows - but why was it called this? Additionally, there is an exedra and a rustic hermitage. A lead statue of Pan by Van Nost which stood on a plinth by the Cold Bath may have been a presiding *genius loci,* since a local cult of the pagan god existed, suggested by a whimsical interpretation of the place-name 'Painswick' as *Pan's Wyck.* This was reinforced by Pan having a special place in garden iconography as a Classical figure representing a Gothick mood.

The intricate rococo style of the garden was expensive to maintain, and soon became unfashionable as the landscape style of 'Capability' Brown evolved, though this one never seems to have been determinedly swept away, just allowed to decline slowly as buildings decayed and piecemeal simplification eroded its complexity. The rococo pattern probably lasted until the early nineteenth century when some alterations were made. It continued unchanged until the 1960s when the garden was abandoned and the site planted as a coniferous wood. Robins's views and the few remaining buildings were left as the only record of its original appearance. The garden became derelict, laying as wilderness.

Then its fortune returned. Realisation that the bones of a rococo garden survived here as nowhere else led the owner in 1984 to start a programme of restoration as close as possible to the original. The site was cleared, and, despite doubts of Robins's painting, recent examination has established in detail the veracity of his remarkable views, certainly sufficient to guide restorative work.

Eagle House

STROUD

Location On the A46 and A419, seven miles south of Gloucester. Sheet 162 85100541

The location of Stroud at the convergence of five valleys helped to make it the industrial centre of the Cotswolds from the seventeenth century but, as too often, it has been spoiled by unprepossessing commercial and speculative building. However, the area did not escape entirely the projection of eccentric imagination, for a sprinkling of interesting follies and other buildings can be found among the Stroudwater valleys.

In Castle Street, overlooking the valley, the garden of an eighteenth-nineteenth-century house known as The Castle contains a sham castle with two castellated towers, one round and one square, linked by a curtain wall. The old part of The Castle was built by Simon and Jane Chadwell in 1610 and it has been enlarged and improved since. It is not known though when or why it acquired its name, nor when the actual sham castle was built, though it must have been a considerable undertaking of interest - or amusement - to the local community. However, there is a tradesman's token of the time of Charles II having *'Henry Allen, of the'* as its obverse, and *'Castel in Stroud'* as its reverse. So which came first: did the sham follow, at the whim of an owner, or did it give the house its name?

In Paganhill, Field Place derives its name from the Field family who were its owners from the fourteenth to the eighteenth centuries. By the failure of their male line, it passed to John Delafield Phelps, whose descendants leased it at the end of the eighteenth century to James Tyers. What the observer now sees is built in eighteenth-century 'Strawberry Hill Gothick' style. The plan, a central range with cross-wings, appears to be derived from that of a late-sixteenth-century house, presumably the one which had nine hearths recorded in 1672, and much of the fabric is probably incorporated into the present structure. However, before 1803 James Tyers gave the house a new south front with embattled parapets and a mix of Gothick and Tudor Revival windows, and the central three-storey, semi-octagonal porch/gazebo was added with its projecting upper storey of blind quatrefoils.

The Castle   *Field Place*

Directly above the town to the south stands a conspicuous landmark. Rodborough Fort is not a country house but a massive and solid sham castle, an inhabited folly first built by Captain Hawker in 1761 as an eyecatcher on a piece of land taken out of Rodborough Common, *'on common land granted by the Lord of the Manor.'* Although it was originally called Fort George, it was later said to have

> *...none of the medieval appearance of the present fort being low and squat...its only claim to the title was a bastion on which stood a battery of cannon placed there by Captain Hawker.*

The original Fort was recorded only once, in a painting attributed to Hawker's son, which depicts a single-storey, five-bay building with a canted centre and Gothick windows.

The Fort passed through the hands of a number of prominent Stroud businessmen before being bought in 1868 by Alexander Holcombe. In 1869-70 he employed a Gloucester architect, A W Maberley, to convert it into a house, when it was rebuilt as a rock-faced but otherwise picturesque Gothick toy fort; the lop-sided gateway which contributes so much to its appearance was added in 1873.

In attempting to create the desired effect, the Fort displays a full range of artefaces, with round, square, straight, battered and machicolated towers and walls, the square towers having particularly heavy battlements, a taller stair turret, and arrow cross-slits. Certainly it is big and noticeable, but despite the variety it is in appearance a folly of pedestrian imagination, failing lamentably as a *'Picturesque'* object.

In recent decades it has been neglected, even changing hands three times in the 1980s. The current owner is though making considerable effort in its rehabilitation.

Amberley Eyecatcher   *Location* Sheet 162 84910218

In 1651, John Stephens of Lypiatt bought a house and fifty-one acres at Rodborough from the Sheppard family of Minchinhampton, which formed the basis of the Rodborough Manor estate, known initially as Hill Living, then as Hill House, and from the late nineteenth century by the present name. The estate changed hands a number of times in the early eighteenth century before being bought in 1757 by a successful Woodchester clothier, Onesipherous Paul, who built a villa here. Paul, knighted in 1760 and created a baronet in 1762, bequeathed the estate to his son of the same name in 1774. The second Sir Onesipherous Paul took the additional Christian name of George in 1780, when he served as High Sheriff, and as Sir George Onesipherous Paul went on to pursue a distinguished career as Chairman of Quarter Sessions and prison reformer of national significance. In 1784-92 he made major alterations to the house and grounds to the designs of Anthony Teck at a cost of £7,185 5s 8d.

The situation of the house on the edge of Rodborough Common gave it spectacular views, and these were complimented by careful landscaping. A broad shelter belt ran round the perimeter of the ornamental grounds, and through it ran a sinuous Shady Walk, leading to a Gothick archway which also formed a folly eyecatcher from the house. Constructed as two plump, round towers with two-light Gothick windows and cross-slits, embattled in between, it is a delightful *'object'*. It survives though now as a private house, with the considerable arch filled in by a big window at the bottom; at the time of the conversion, the castellations of the towers were also filled in, but those on the curtain wall remain.

The architect was probably Anthony Teck, although the whole structure looks Sanderson Miller-ish. It is referred to as 'the Amberley eyecatcher', though it is actually situated in the hamlet of St. Chloe. The best view of it now is from the A46 below, though it is difficult to identify as it hides against the hillside amongst trees. From Sir George's house it must have been a focus of considerable interest.

CHALFORD

Location One mile east of Stroud, on the A419. Sheet 163 89310247

This was cloth producing country. The village is situated on the northern slopes of the Golden Valley, so steep in places that many roads are unsuitable for motor traffic - yet, somehow, pack animals were expected to carry their loads up and down them. It was an industrial centre, its water-powered mills grinding corn and fulling cloth long before the Industrial Revolution brought even greater propserity. It was through this busy valley that the cloth was transported from Stroud to London for export overseas, through which the canal was later built and then superseded by the railways.

'Gazebo' is a mock-Latin word of the eighteenth century which with its future ending seems to have evolved as a synonym for the Italian-named belvedere ('pleasant view') on top of a house. Sometimes it was used of garden belvederes or prospect towers, but gazebo, for 'a gazing place', is now commonly applied to those small fanciful buildings or rooms perched at the corner of a garden wall to give a view of the road or the country on the other side. They were pleasant places for resting, watching the passing of public or private coaches, or waiting for a first glimpse of arriving friends. They belong to a quieter, horse-drawn age when traffic was an event, but for some reason are now often neglected.

In the district quaintly known as *Old Neighbourhood,* the former clothier's large house named *Sevillowes* has a very steep garden laid out in terraces made for hanging out cloth to dry. At the very top is a lovely Gothick gazebo, with ogee windows and doorway, under a curved pediment, and is certainly a step nearer to a folly than the average summer house. Parts of the man-made terraces are held up on arches with rooms behind, a further legacy of their former function.

NORTH NIBLEY

Location Nine miles south-west of Stroud, off the B4060. Sheet 162 74329563

In a commanding position on the wooded Knoll high above the village of North Nibley, 650 feet above sea level, is a tapering stone tower, Gloucestershire's tallest, standing one hundred and eleven feet high and twenty-six-and-a-half feet square at the bottom, with stairs leading to a gallery. It is visible for miles around and commands a breathtaking view across the Severn plain and the Forest of Dean to the distant Black Mountains of Wales.

This is a monument to the memory of William Tyndale, one of the great controversial clerics of the Reformation and who was the first person to translate the New Testament into English. Tyndale was born in 1484, possibly at North Nibley. After ordination in 1521 he obtained the post of tutor to the two sons of Sir John Walsh, himself in the service of Henry VIII, at Little Sodbury Manor, and was thoroughly shocked by the ignorance and prejudices of the local clergy, with whom he argued openly. Since his tutorial duties were not at all demanding he went round neighbouring churches preaching his views. On hearing of this behaviour, the Bishop of Gloucester's Chancellor summoned him and in Tyndale's words,

> *... threatened me grievously and revyled and rated me as though*
> *I had been a dogge.*

For the benefit of his pupils at Little Sodbury, Tyndale had translated Erasmus' *Enchyridion,* which he prefaced with a vigorous diatribe against the vices of the clergy. Here he also thought out the future translation of the New Testament, and is said to have addressed the following words, which made him famous, to an opponent in debate in the Great Hall of Little Sodbury Manor:

> *If God spare my life, ere many years I will cause a boy that driveth*
> *the plough shall know more of the scripture than thou doest!*

Still Sir John Walsh supported him, but thought it prudent to pass him on to another patron. In 1523 Tyndale moved to London where he lived with a wealthy draper, Humphrey Monmouth. Working from the Greek and Hebrew, he began the task of translating the New Testament into English. This, together with his outspoken views, brought him into conflict with the Church hierarchy and to escape persecution he fled to Europe. In 1525 Tyndale began printing his translation, first at Cologne and later at Worms. Many of the printed copies were smuggled back into England on merchant ships and found a ready sale, but any discovered by the authorities were burnt. It is interesting to note that, almost 500 years ago, Tyndale referred to divinity with a gender-neutral pronoun:

> *All thyngs were made by it / and without it/*
> *was made noo thinge / that made was.*
> *In it was lyfe.*

He spent the next few years in Antwerp but in 1535, at the instigation of Henry VIII, was arrested and incarcerated in a dungeon at Vilvorde, near Brussels, There he remained for exactly five hundred days before being found guilty of heresy. The punishment was terrible: he was ceremoniously stripped of his priest's vestments, executed by strangulation, and his body burned.

Politics in those days were even more convoluted than today. Two years before Tyndale was martyred, the Convocation of Canterbury petitioned Henry VIII that the whole Bible might be translated into English. The following year, Miles Coverdale (1488-1568), an Augustinian friar and reformer who, like Tyndale, had been forced to reside abroad, produced the first complete English Bible, which he dedicated to the King. Wherever possible, Coverdale followed Tyndale's work, but much of the Old Testament he translated from the German of Martin Luther (1483-1546) and others.

With the excuse - as good as any - that William Tyndale had been born in North Nibley 382 years earlier, and the existence of a perfect site for a tower clearly visible from his new estate at Tortworth, the monument was opened by Lord Ducie on 6 November, 1866. Also in attendance on that inaugural day was the Revd. David Edwards, whom we shall meet again.

Once described as *"unspeakably ugly sleazily tapering"*, this tall, tapering, stone belvedere tower with a pyramidal roof plus cross was designed by Samuel S Teulon, and the enamel work undertaken by Salviati, with the inscription:

> *Erected AD 1866 in grateful remembrance of William Tyndale,*
> *translator of the English Bible who first caused the New Testament*
> *to be printed in the mother tongue of his countrymen; born near*
> *this spot, he suffered martyrdom at Vilvorde in Flanders, on*
> *6th October, 1536.*

How accurate is the claim of *'this spot'* to be the birth-place? Nearby is Tyndale Cottage, which is certainly old enough, but there are other claimants: Wotton-under-Edge has been put forward as a possiblity, as has Hurst Farmhouse at Slimbridge. Biographical information in the sixteenth century being as unreliable as it is, there is more than a probability that the William Tyndale who lived at North Nibley at the beginning of the century was not the same as the William Tyndale whose birthplace was almost certainly *'on the borders of Wales'* and who translated the Bible - in which case the monument is pure folly.

STINCHCOMBE

Location Eight miles south-west of Stroud, on the B4060. Sheet 162 73879680

Stancombe Park is a little-known house with a wonderful garden, so placed on the side of Stinchcombe Hill as to have both a south aspect and a view of the main Cotswold ridge. Originally built for P B Purnell in the second decade of the nineteenth century, in 1886 the house was mostly rebuilt in the same late-Georgian style with insurance money after a fire - but the distant garden and two 'Picturesque' cottages remained intact: built of bright yellow stone, with gables and panels of diagonally-worked red brick, the roofs curve as a Far-Eastern pagoda but the chimneys are richly Tudor and there is a lot of Cotswold detail, as if the builder had interpreted a drawing from a pattern-book on village architecture. Below and some distance to the south of the house, in the hollow of the Park, is the garden laid out in the romantic tradition sometime in the nineteenth century, encompassing every exotic ingredient of such a tradition, winding walks, fine trees, pavilions and a temple, subterranean tunnels and gloomy grottos, a hidden lake and mossy cascades, the pagoda-like cottages, Egyptian and pre-historic themes.

When was it built? This is a difficult question. It lies just into North Nibley parish, for which no maps survive to indicate the date of its creation. The opinion that it dates from 'the late nineteenth century' cannot be sustained and even the alternative suggestion of c.1840 seems a little late.

If we cannot set a date to it, do we know why it was built? Here fiction takes over. Too recent to be a legend, the story of the vicar's Secret Garden smacks of rumour. In the mid-nineteenth century Miss Purnell, who owned Stancombe Park, married the Revd. Edwards, vicar of North Nibley. He set about creating a romantic garden far from the house where, so the story goes, without being observed he could have assignations with a gypsy woman who was his one true love. In practicality, he must have spent very considerable periods of time away from the house planning, designing and supervising the pathways, cascades, grottos, temples, water-works and all the other impedimenta deemed essential to the creation of a mood. There is no doubt, though, the mood he achieved eventually was romantic in the extreme: any gypsy with fire in her blood would have capitulated immediately.

The house, looking earlier than 1840 but actually later, is a jewel. The site is magnificent, at the head of one of the most beautiful naturally landscaped valleys in England. The house is built high and from it a dark romantic glen falls through ferns and rhododendrons. An iron-fenced path winds gently downhill below the immaculate main garden, looking high and over the valley to the Tyndale monument, and down to a small lake in the valley with an island reached by a Chinese bridge. On the path from the formal to the romantic garden is a zoo of topiary: both Bactrian and Dromedary camels, pigs, dogs, monkeys and a gentle serpent, line the way, their unseeing eyes guarding the path, directing visitors' eyes ever downwards. As the path gives way to steps so the mood changes from serenity to mystery; we are aware of the sound of rushing water, the air becomes humid, the atmosphere torrid. At the bottom, traces of a round flower-bed mark the centre of a glade of pines.

Topiary

Suddenly the path becomes paths - there are stone-flagged paths everywhere, a multiple-choice garden. The main one passes a grotto, and then leads into abrupt darkness, goes into a tunnel under the old drive, emerges briefly into the light giving enough time for a huge white stone dog to startle visitors, then plunges into blackness again, an apparent cul-de-sac but for a pin-point of light at the end. Water drips traditionally ahead and we pass a little slit through which a thin cascade can be seen.

Everywhere is so narrow that the walls seem to enclose the explorer. The dark path turns left and goes out up steps onto a rough path, but quickly into another grotto, another skimpily-rocked entrance to coffin-narrow passages of plain, untextured, practical brick. A hundred and fifty years have spread a thin yellow-green stain over some of the walls; otherwise they are smooth and bare, with no sign at all of more romantic intentions.

Egyptian Doorway

The chink looks out over the lake, running north and south, an irregular oval almost 150 yards long, the edges grown with rushes, lilies and willow-herb, huge oaks, copper-beech, chestnut and mountain-ash with ferns everywhere. And a huge stone boar looks back from across the lake. Four tunnels meet. High in the vaulting is a round eye of green light which shows another dark door into the nettles and a spare vaulted niche with pantry shelves, its whitewash and mirror back lightening the gloom to display a collection of shells, ammonites and fossils.

Here the path divides. The left returns us to daylight on the other long side of the lake, leading round under a pergola-covered lakeside walk; the right to another underground junction, where a straight path, so closely hedged in that only the charming perspective down the sunny flags is visible, with arches of iron overhead to centre the eye, leads to what is the most memorable part of the garden, the end of the vista, a small square court, enclosed on three sides, with a plain, bare urn in the centre and an exotic doorway breaking the walls on each side, one a whale-bone arch, one a Cretan doorway with curved lintel, and the third an extraordinary affair like a keyhole or an Egyptian ankh. These doorways stay in the mind long after leaving this garden. The Stonehenge-shaped one on the left frames a winding path leading to a seat under a tree, the only place on this side from which the lake is visible, a nice touch of skill. The Moorish door is completely undecorated but leads through a black passage to a narrow path

West Pavilion

flanked by flawless, castellated hedges of thick box, round the south-west foot of the lake and past a massive whale's skull, ending at the Temple, overlooking the water, a small golden-stoned Tuscan eyecatcher or summer-house ignorant of the punctiliousness of true Classical architecture. The steps from the Temple go down through that uniform grey-green tangle into which formal beds always disintegrate, to a semi-circle of stone jutting into the lake, enclosing a little pond with a fountain. Crumbs call up enormous goldfish.

At the far end of the Temple walk is an open square of flower-beds enclosed in a trellis cage whose piers are crowned with wooden steeples. On two sides of it are little leaded-glass pavilions, like Tweedledee and Tweedledum, guarding the corner, with fairy-tale roofs. Inside they have narrow shelves in stadium rows for a display of the parti-coloured, fringed and curled elaborations of hot-house flowers. One pavilion has a fountain, and another fountain stands in the centre of the square, with birds bending their heads to support on their looped necks a basin, in which stand more birds and, on their smaller necks, a smaller basin.

So we return to the question: why was the garden built? Does the traditional explanation have any validity? Could all this have been created by a love-torn vicar? The romantic garden may be remote and invisible from the house, but it is next to the main road and is flanked by servants' cottages; moreover the old main drive to the house runs right over the garden and is used as a landscape feature. In reality, it is difficult to see how the Revd. Edwards could have managed to hold the secret assignations as the garden would have been filled constantly with workmen building the features and planting. It is even possible that the garden predated him and was built about 1820 by people now unknown but according to one local story who had learned the motifs from soldiers who had served in the Egyptian campaigns of the Napoleonic Wars. Whatever, Stancombe is certainly one of the most satisfying of gardens.

As one might expect, there are differing opinions about Stancombe. Certainly every ingredient of a romantic garden is here, and is more than one hundred and fifty years old, but, according to one critic, *"everything is wrong, thin and entirely unmellowed"*. For example, the urn in the little court is the focal point of a long perspective from one direction, and from the other it is the first thing visible from a dark passage, yet it has neither interesting detail nor elegance of shape. Was it designed by someone who knew what was wanted but not quite how? It succeeds though in evoking shudders and surprises, and more than most romantic gardens it offers sudden shifts from gentle melancholy to sunny cheerfulness. It certainly stays in the mind for long after leaving.

On the other hand, Stancombe is transitional. The choice of location for the house at the head of a pretty valley, the flowing, informal landscaping and planting, the use of cottages with their chalet air as part of the design, the building of exotic conceits, all belong to the Romantic tradition. The enclosure of the lake in a tight belt of garden; the beds, theatres, and pavilions for flowers; the static tightness of the fountains; the choice of Egyptian and prehistoric themes for the conceits instead of Chinese; the gravel and elaborate herbaceous borders: all these anticipate the second half of the nineteenth century. Here is beauty and romanticism, as gardens provided before, but with a changed focus, the eye looking close instead of across the valley, not at a plantation but at a rose.

After a period of neglect, new owners have cleared and replanted the garden. The Temple has been renovated. The novel topiary has been added. The formal garden at the top of the hollow, beside the house, has been returned to its former magnificence. All augurs well for Stancombe's secret garden. - which remains very private and not open to casual visitors.

Shell Grotto

68

WOODCHESTER

Location Off the B4066, three miles south-west of Stroud. Sheet 162 80930148

In 1845, the 4,000 acre estate of the 2nd Earl Ducie was put up for sale. The purchaser was William Leigh. Son of a successful merchant who had made a fortune from trading in Liverpool, Leigh had been left a huge inheritance, including a shipowning and trading company in Liverpool, considerable property, and interests in Australia. Acting on the advice of Augustus Pugin he bought and then demolished the Ducie's Georgian-style Spring Park. Following his reception into the Roman Catholic Church a year earlier at the age of forty-two, Leigh had promoted his new faith with enthusiasm and generosity and resolved to move to a place receptive to his intention to set up monastic institutions. Woodchester offered this ideal environment.

Leigh went to live in a modest house always known locally as The Cottage (though it has sixteen bedrooms) and turned his attention to his main project, the founding of a Catholic community. He commissioned the architect Charles Hansom (brother of the inventor of the Hansom cab), who was cheaper than Pugin, to design a monastery for the Passionist Fathers sited in the village of Woodchester; work began in 1846 and was completed in 1849. As a foretaste of things to come, the cost was £9,000 which can be compared to that of the nearby parish church, almost two decades later, of £3,400.

Leigh commissioned Pugin to draw up a scheme for a new house, but rejected the designs and baulked at the projected cost, and their association ended in acrimony. One of Hansom's assistants was Benjamin Bucknall, a local boy, son of a clothier from Rodborough, and brought up in a background of mill engineering. He was deeply interested in architectural practice, especially in the ideas of the French theorist Eugene Viollet-le-Duc, whose friend and translator he later became. Under Hansom, Bucknall acquired architectural expertise so quickly that when in 1854 Leigh revived his plan for a new house, it was Bucknall, still only twenty-one years of age, whom he commissioned.

Leigh instructed his young architect to take the drawings done by Pugin (who had died two years earlier) as his guide, and the house which evolved resembles in many ways those first sketches; yet Bucknall produced a masterful design of his own, quite different in style from other Gothic Revival buildings of the same period. Here was a golden opportunity to employ the theories of Viollet-le-Duc: Bucknall took that opportunity.

There is no stranger house in Gloucestershire. Work was begun sometime around late 1856 and for fourteen years the house slowly took shape. The reason for this leisurely rate of building is unclear but may be linked to Leigh's parsimony. The date on the clock-tower - 1858 - shows that early work was well-advanced. After that, however, it slowed down. Two dates incised inside by workmen - 1862 and 1866 with the initials 'A.T.' - record the progress. By now the roof had been tiled and the bells installed in the tower. The work began to stutter to a halt. A datestone on the tower reads 1872: shortly after that, worked stopped altogether.

From the outset the house was meant to be a domestic version of a Roman Catholic community: worship came before comfort and convenience, and as an expression of Leigh's monastic fervour it would have been ideal. The house clearly resembles a medieval church, with its buttresses, traceried windows and gargoyles. Looking at the south-west corner, one cannot fail to be struck by the monstrous stone gargoyles, projecting horizontally from the face of the south range. These look like pure decoration but in fact have a functional purpose: they are part of the drainage system, and being hollow act as chutes to throw rainwater clear of the building. In the same way, the buttresses are essential to the structure, designed to balance the large areas of window and to counteract the outward thrust of the arched and vaulted ceilings within. A chapel featured prominently, projecting from the east range, and the design included everything to make the establishment self-sufficient: bakery, brewery, cheese-room, laundry, and so on. Leigh's dream was not only to live in a medieval building but to return to a simple, monastic and medieval form of existence.

Bucknall's chosen medium was stone - mainly the warm, creamy limestone which came from local quarries - and he used it for almost every part of the building: not only for the outer walls, staircases, ceiling vaults, door-surrounds and fireplaces, but also for the bath, the main drainage-pipes and the gutters, pipes and chutes of the rainwater system. The level of skill of the masons was extremely high, and some of the carving is at least as good as any in medieval buildings. The enormouse soil-pipe descending from the principal lavatory represents the ultimate in stone technology, being eighteen inches in diameter. The turret-like roof of the clock tower is carved from stone to resemble slates.

The front door opens directly into the hall - marked on Bucknall's plans as a billiards room - and the visitor is confronted immediately by the unfinished state of the interior. Above the hall there are no ceilings at either first or second floor, so one can see straight up some fifty feet to the roof. Many details of Bucknall's construction methods are apparent. A great deal of fine stonework has been completed, fireplace, door-surrounds, skirting, which stand nearly an inch proud of the walls ready for the plaster to bring them flush with the finished surfaces. A particularly fascinating feature is the fan-shaped springing, already built into the walls, which would have carried the vaulted ceiling. High overhead a sweeping stone arch bears the purlins which support the roof - a feature common in churches but most unusual in a private house. At ground level, the windows are framed by both front and rear arches of stone, with a deep groove between them to accommodate curtains.

View from Dining Room

Other rooms are in the same unfinished state. The showpiece of the dining room is the centering, or curved wooden framework, still in position beneath a brick arch. The wood - probably pine - is in good condition, preserved for the 130 years by the excellent ventilation. The brickwork above the centering is finished: a few more days, and the scaffolding would have come down. Are the Victorian builders still here? Was their exit so unexpected and sudden? Why did they leave the thirty-foot wooden ladder propped against the wall? Why the small sheets of protective boarding fixed to guard exposed stonework against possible damage from falling debris? It all adds to a strange sense of immediacy.

The drawing room is the most splendid, and the only one to have been finished, for a visit by Cardinal Vaughan in 1894. The wooden floor, the surfaces finely plastered flush with the stonework, the windows glazed with simple, uncoloured leaded panes, the ceiling containing more than fifty carved stone bosses of the highest quality, the lovely stone vaulting - all give an idea of how the rest of the house would finally have looked.

The chapel is the grandest part of the whole building, with its soaring lines and splendid stone-vaulted ceiling. The west window is fashioned in stone tracery as a circle within a triangle - a symbolic shape beloved of Victorians. Set into the chapel walls are two elevated galleries. That on the south has access from the first-floor corridor, and was designed so that the master of the house could attend devotions from a private vantage-point. The gallery opposite, for the servants, is set on a lower level; but its carved stone decoration, which the master would have been able to see, is more elaborate than that on the front of his own gallery, which was out of his sight. Beyond the chapel the sacristy has a small stone confessional built into the wall, and a half-carved gargoyle standing abandoned on the dusty floor!

A temporary wooden staircase leads up to the first floor and the fascinating bathroom. The bath is carved from a single block of stone; the hot and cold water inlets are a pair of stone gargoyles, and the taps which fed them could be controlled by a servant in the next room! Had he laid in the bath, Leigh could have contemplated the fine carving on the mantelpiece, one side showing birds pecking at acorns, the other a serpent among forbidden fruit.

Unfinished building

Stone technology extends also to the attendant shower room (surely an innovation for those days) - big enough to take a dozen bathers at once; the two water inlets overhead, shaped as leopards' heads, were probably designed to direct hot and cold flows into a single stream, but we will never know whether or not the system would have been efficient.

There is a great mystery of Woodchester Park Mansion: why was it never finished? That the builders left behind their scaffolding and wooden arch centering has led to the tradition they decamped in a hurry. The reality is less sensational. There was not an abrupt end to the work – the men did not down tools and leave overnight. Stone masons were still working here, albeit at a very reduced rate, in 1872. What tools they did not take with them were disposed of at a sale in 1873, lasting three days.

The Mansion was only one of Leigh's projects in the area. The first had been the monastery and church for the Dominican Order. He gave land for the Convent in 1860, and also set about refurbishing the farm houses and barns on the Woodchester estate, many with the same massive solidity evident in the Mansion. This extensive programme of reconstruction stretched both his financial and his human resources. The lay-off at the Mansion was caused in part by Leigh transferring his main interest, and most of his men, to the Convent.

Moreover, Leigh's health was already failing, and his doctors advised against living in this great stone masterpiece, too cold and on a damp site, down in the valley. Perhaps he could not foresee the building being completed for him and his reduced family to inhabit, for his two daughters had already died, childless. But the most likely explanation of why the Mansion was never finished is that William Leigh simply ran out of money. He remained at The Cottage, where, in January, 1873, at the age of seventy, he died, leaving a colossal white elephant three hundred feet below.

After Leigh's death his son, William, his only remaining child, always known as 'Squire' Leigh, returned from Australia but, not sharing his father's religious compulsions, did nothing towards finishing the intended house: in his opinion the estate was too small to support a house that size - and he wasted no money on it.

However, though incomplete, Woodchester Mansion must rank as one of the great achievements of nineteenth century architecture, a remarkable synthesis of French Gothic Revival and the local Cotswold tradition. It was all begun to accommodate a family and servants who never came. If ever a house deserves to be called a folly, this one does.

HAWKESBURY UPTON

Location East of A46, eighteen miles south-west of Cirencester. Sheet 172 77588702

Lord Edward Somerset, one of Wellington's Major-Generals, had a long and distinguished military career befitting a son of the Duke of Beaufort of nearby Badminton. Such was his gallantry when serving at Waterloo that he received the official thanks of Parliament. When he died in 1842 at the age of 66, his friends decided to erect a commemorative monument and work began on it soon afterwards. This towers above the village of Hawkesbury, itself sitting beneath the wooded escarpment.

The tall, stone tower, rather Chinese- or Indian-looking, with a barbaric portcullis and chain-railing round the top, was designed by Lewis Vulliamy, one of the more fashionable early-Victorian architects. In his mastery of the Gothic, he was said to have been *"far in advance of his contemporaries"*, so it is a puzzle why the style of the tower, particularly the ornate stone-work on the roof, seems more Eastern than anything else: neither Somerset nor Vulliamy had any connection with China or India. As if to excuse this heathen decoration the top of the tower is surmounted by a large cross. Inside the doorway a marble slab records the valiant daring-do of Lord Somerset.

Though altogether a bleak piece of design with some gilding, this tower is a rarity amongst follies: it is easily accessible and in excellent condition. Quite obviously, the location was selected for the views it provides. There is a caveat to be added: those prepared to take advantage of the damp but solid spiral staircase leading to the balcony should be aware that the wind here can be phenomenal!

GREAT BADMINTON

Location West of B4040, nineteen miles south-west of Tetbury. Sheet 173 81278386

For four hundred years, from the mid-thirteenth century, Badminton was owned by the Boteler family, many members of which were prominent in public office in Gloucestershire, several of whom were knighted, and one of whom is immortalised as a gargoyle on Winchcombe parish church. Despite occasional reversals, they continued as successful gentry into the sixteenth century, when successive generations married into other county families like the Guises of Elmore, the Newtons and the Youngs. By the early seventeenth century, however, Nicholas Boteler was in financial difficulties and was obliged to sell Badminton. Although he offered the Berkeleys an option on the property, in 1608 it was bought by Edward, 4th Earl of Worcester, who was looking for an estate to settle on his second son, Thomas Somerset, who promptly transformed it into a Jacobean mansion, and in 1616 married the dowager Countess of Ormonde. Thomas's unmarried daughter succeeded him and on her death in 1655 left it to her second cousin, Henry, Lord Herbert (1629-1700), later 3rd Marquess of Worcester (succeeded 1667), later 1st Duke of Beaufort (created 1682).

Until then the Lords Worcester had lived at Raglan Castle in Monmouthshire, which was acquired by the 1st Earl's wife in her own right as Lady Herbert of Raglan. The gift of Badminton was very welcome since Raglan Castle had been 'slighted' by the Parliamentarians during the Civil Wars. The Earl's father had been a staunch 'King's man' who suffered grievously for his loyalty; he was also a man of rare inventiveness who published a book in which the power and application of the steam engine are described, and who nearly succeeded in making an artificial bird fly, chirp and even hover. Indeed, both Lord Herbert's father and grandfather had been fervent Royalists who between them were reputed to have spent over £900,000 on the royalist cause.

The Somerset estates were seized by Parliament, but when Lord Herbert came of age in 1650 he set about repairing the ruined family fortunes. He became an MP and a personal friend of Cromwell, renounced Catholicism and successfully pushed his claim to the family estates, which were mostly back in his hands by the time he inherited Badminton in 1655. In 1657 he married a wealthy widow, Lady Beauchamp, and at the Restoration he transferred his support successfully to Charles II. Under the new regime he was a rising star, becoming a Privy Councillor, and Lord President of the Council of Wales in 1672 before being rewarded with a Dukedom ten years later for loyalty to the Stuart cause. He held Bristol against the Duke of Monmouth in 1685 and against William of Orange in 1688, and although he was reconciled with William, who visited him at Badminton in 1690, he remained in political retirement until his death in 1700.

It was as the 3rd Marquess that he began transforming the Botelers' rambling and gabled house into a palace. This was an early essay at the Palladian style and if not by Inigo Jones may have been designed by his assistant, John Webb, although it is equally likely that the Marquess himself may have been responsible. Evidently though, the Marquess's chief concern was his park. Licences to enlarge the originally modest area were obtained from Cromwell in 1648 and from Charles II in 1664, and exchanges and conveyances for the purpose started in 1658 and continued to the end of the century. The flat terrain enabled him to work on a gigantic scale. He made the house the nucleus of a great wheel of thirty straight rides radiating out across the countryside, which were intersected by some twenty-four others radiating from a *rond-point* to the south-east. In 1699 Celia Fiennes recorded that from the roof of the house it was possible to

> *...look twelve ways down to ye parishes and grounds between all*
> *through glides or vistos of trees.*

The symbolism could not have been stronger. Whether intended or not, the avenues were a potent image of the way in which the Duke's influence radiated out across his estates and far beyond. The designer of this grand scheme is not known for certain, but was probably John Mansfield who between 1683 and 1688 was receiving payments as the gardener.

The Duke's network of straight rides has been smudged by the changes of time rather than by the positive hands of improvers, yet several of them remain intact and others can still be traced, notably the drive from the north entrance of the house to Worcester Lodge, a dead-straight avenue nearly three miles long that ends at the arch of the most beautiful lodge in England. The extraordinary layout fascinated neighbouring landowners. Roger North recorded that

> *...divers gentlemen cut their trees and hedges to humour his vistos,*
> *and some planted their hills in his line, for compliment, at their*
> *own charge.*

The Duke died in 1700. His elder son having predeceased him (killed after throwing himself out of a runaway coach), he was succeeded by his grandson. The 2nd Duke, a strong Tory and Jacobite sympathizer, survived only fourteen years, having achieved little in the building line though he spent £20,000 on furniture and pictures which had still not reached Badminton when he died. His chief impact on the park is Swangrove, a fanciful *maison de plaisance* on its edge, some two miles north of the house, off the Dunkirk road. Designed c.1703 either by Sumsion of Colerne or by William Killigrew, it is a self-consciously rustic but elegant rendering of the 'Cotswold Revival' tradition on a minute scale, with mullioned and transomed windows and gables. Originally no more than a pavilion, it seems to have been planned for excursions, and had an elegant panelled room with adjacent buffet; a more intimate upper panelled room, decorated with marbling and chinoiserie and approached by outside steps, was added later in the century. To complete the picture there are four tiny detached pavilions, one at each corner of the garden. Alongside Swangrove is a little castellated barn with hipped roof.

Castellated Barn

75

The 2nd Duke's son, the 3rd Duke, combined a love of sport with the arts, and seems to have inherited his great-grandfather's architectural interests. To complete the interior remodelling of the House he engaged the Tory and Catholic architect James Gibbs, though it is open to question whether the great entrance hall, intended to take the canvases by John Wootton of the 3rd Duke depicted beagling, hawking, racing and stag-hunting, and of his life-size white Arabian horse over the fireplace, is to Gibbs's design. At all events the hall is one of the noblest state-rooms in the Cotswolds. It was here during a particularly inclement winter in 1863 that the children of the 8th Duke invented the game of badminton, and to this day the game retains the same dimensions as this north entrance hall.

When the 3rd Duke died in 1745, his brother was quick to discard Gibbs in favour of William Kent who was brought to Badminton at first to advise on the gardens and then to alter the north front. Kent's main contribution was Worcester Lodge, the combined entrance gate and banqueting pavilion that stands three miles due north of the house on the furthest perimeter of the park, and is yet in full view of it. Acclaimed as one of Kent's best designs, the Lodge was built after his death under the direction of his clerk of works, Stephen Wright, and finished in 1750 at a cost of £721. In 1754, the peripatetic Bishop Pococke of Ossory recorded in his diary a visit to Badminton, *'Worcester Lodge, on the highest ground of the park, is a design by Kent. It is a grand room where the duke dines in summer'*. What an understatement! Both park guardian and park focus, the Lodge is at once an archetype of the grand gate lodge and an eyecatcher that upstages the main house. It has been described as *"...a compressed palace rather than ... a garden house..."* whose *'...architectural symbolism is brutally direct: the low pyramidal pavilions house the servants, the high domed room over the arch is for the duke'*. Over the arch, the interior of the Lodge consists of a lofty, sumptuously decorated banqueting room reached by a stone staircase enclosed on one side of the gateway arch; the other side houses the service pantry. A splendid gilded overmantel mirror with a faceted sunburst is contemporary with the decoration of the room.

Worcester Lodge

Before Kent's death in 1748, a new architectural genius was introduced to Badminton by the Duchess's brother, Norborne Berkeley: This was Thomas Wright of Durham (not known as a relative of his namesake, Stephen), a mysterious person whose first choice of career was as a mathematician and astronomer, in which capacity he achieved great distinction and discovered the Milky Way, and who was at the peak of his powers when the desertion and death of many of his patrons forced him to turn to architectural and landscape design.

'I am sorry the stars have used you ill', wrote William Cowper, who had a cynical view of those in the fashionable world who had at first lauded and then abandoned his friend. He mocked that Wright's celestial erudition had been but

> *... laying a lane before them which concentrated all their greatness into an atom ... Now you lay before them their own greatness, and what is really the fruit of your genius shall hereafter be shown as the contrivance and art of the great proprietor.*

Wright worked at Badminton for thirty-six years, producing for the *'great proprietors'* Charles, 4th Duke, and then Henry, 5th Duke, a quantity of fanciful castellated and rustic buildings, many of which unfortunately have disappeared.

For the eighteenth-century proprietor, intrigued by nature and the 'gothic' past, the hermit was a cult-figure, and the hermitage a construction or excavation in keeping with the spirit of his landscape garden. Fashion and their ephemeral materials have swept away most of the dark caves of solitude which could be found on gentlemen's parks but at Badminton the Root House or Hermit's Cell is the largest surviving example of the once-popular hermitage. Designed by Wright in 1747, it is an astonishing work made entirely of off-cuts of logs of wood and tree roots. The Cell is wonderfully preserved, a fine room rather than a cell, oddly placed in the open deer-park without a rock and only a few trees in sight (though not melancholy yews as contemporary fashion dictated); perhaps the park was more wooded when it was constructed two centuries ago.

Root House or Hermit's Cell

This Cell is about twenty-five feet by fourteen feet, with a swooping, thatched roof. A spike on top may be the remains of the cross that completed most hermitages, according to the surviving prints of them. The door-frame is the upturned fork of a huge tree; four more big and particularly knotty trunks make the corner posts, and three more at each end form the steep pediments, which have sections of hollow tree, as *yeux de boeuf,* around iron gratings. At each end is a curved bay with a two-light pointed window, and everywhere is a wild, jumbled in-fill of branches, roots, knots and sawn ends. Under the rear pediment, which is curved, is a branch bench with an ogee back, lettered in nailheads *HERE LOUNGERS LOITER* up one curve, and *HERE THE WEARY REST* down the other. For a thatched building made out of unworked roots and lumps of diseased trees still to be standing after two-and-a-half centuries is an achievement in itself.

There are other follies surviving in the park, all erected between 1748 and 1756 when Thomas Wright was at the height of his genius, and manifestations of the interest in the decorative *'ferme ornee':* together they comprise the most dramatic group of Gothic-style farm buildings. The miniature Ragged Castle, of c.1750, is a charming, extremely ragged little rubble castle, square with one circular turret for the stairs, and the whole crowned with enormous untrimmed slabs of stone for castellations. Kennel Lodge is an octagonal ashlar building with an open balustraded parapet and Tuscan porch. The pair of quaint castellated Slait Lodges have round towers at the four corners and central chimneys, like Staffordshire pottery ornaments found on chimney-pieces. Upper Slait Lodge has Gothic windows, overhanging eaves and a rustic porch. Bath Lodge is different again, in Classical style, in actuality a pair of cottages with pediments, chamfered quoins of alternating lengths, and round-headed enriched windows. The superb battlemented Castle Barn has massive towers, into which are built cartsheds, flanking either side of a screen wall with crow-stepped gable in the centre, which hides a seven-bay barn.

Castle Barn

In 1750 Thomas Wright produced a wonderful Rococo plan for a new garden and over the next few years made designs for a Chinese temple and a Chinese garb for Swangrove. In 1756 the 4th Duke died, leaving yet another minor as heir, and work at Badminton more or less stopped. Payments to Thomas Wright by the 5th Duke are recorded as late as 1768, but after that he did no more work here.

DODINGTON

The medieval manor house of Dodington, which was for many years a parcel of the Berkeley estates, lay in a different location from the present house, but within the park. In 1473 it passed by marriage to Thomas Wekys, and a relative, Robert, began the first house on the current site in 1557; stone from the demolished Dursley Castle was recorded in 1560 as being reused here. In the reign of King James the estate was sold to Giles Codrington, whose family already owned extensive property in the area. Giles' great-great-grandson, Samuel Codrington, sold it to a kinsman, Christopher Codrington, who had made a fortune out of sugar and slaves while Governor of the Leeward Islands, and at his death in 1715 the estate passed to his nephew William, whose descendants retained it until 1984.

In 1728 Alexander Pope described the house as

> *... pretty enough, the situation romantic, covered with woody hills*
> *stumbling upon one another confusedly, and the garden makes a valley*
> *betwixt them with some mounts and waterfalls.*

Sir William Codrington, who inherited at the age of 19 in 1738 and died in 1792, was interested in both architecture and landscape gardening. In 1764 he asked 'Capability' Brown to improve the park, and a considerable amount of woodland was removed to create a large lawn in front of the house (where some of the oldest and best trees were retained) and open up the valleys. Brown also formed two lakes, the upper of which feeds water along an aqueduct carried over a Gothick bridge and down a cascade into the lower. Planting trees in 'natural' positions, digging lakes, making valleys and building hills was an astonishing achievement. Already by September 1766 Mrs Boscawen could report to Lady Chatham:

> *... today visited Dodington, where Mr Brown having been before Us, and*
> *finding great Capabilities of Hills and Vales, shade and Water has*
> *dispos'd of the whole in a scene which greatly excited our Admiration,*
> *and would Yours more as I have a Notion You have seen it in its Ancient*
> *formal Dress: tis really delightful now.*

Altogether, Brown received £1, 368 for his work at Dodington, which was completed in 1767, but this was not the last contribution to the park.

In 1792 Sir William was succeeded not by his son, whom he had disinherited, but by his great-nephew, Christopher, who shared his benefactor's interests in architecture and gardening. The new owner at once called in William Emes and John Webb to make changes to the landscaping which, mainly by additional planting, softened the Brownian landscape.

Christopher Codrington also turned his attention to the house. James Wyatt, then at the height of his career, was appointed architect in 1796 and although by this time the bulk of Wyatt's practice was in the Gothick style, Codrington had him design and build one of the great British neo-Classical houses. The two men became personal friends, and Codrington received better treatment and more assiduous attention than was William Beckford's earlier experience at Fonthill Splendens, from which Wyatt took parts of the Rococo staircase in 1808 and re-erected at Dodington. Despite the great wealth provided by the Codringtons' West Indian estates (they owned Antigua and Barbuda) work proceeded slowly, using mainly estate labour and with the costs being met in most years out of the profits on the English estates. Work on the interior was still in progress in 1813 when James Wyatt was killed in a coaching accident on the Great West Road on his way back to London from a visit to Dodington. Despite the greatest attention to economy and meticulous accounting, however, the size and luxury of the house were such that the overall cost was prodigious. By 1810, nearly £62,000 had been spent on the construction and decoration of the house and the church, which is attached to it by a curved conservatory. The furnishing, which was still being completed in the 1820s, cost a further £60,000. For this fortune, Sir Christopher, as he became in 1816, achieved the grandest house in the county, if not the west of England.

It is not clear whether the Gothick arch and cascade buildings were designed by 'Capability' Brown about 1764 or are a later alteration by James Wyatt, but in either case they are not successful as pleasure buildings. A waterfall passes through the central pointed arch of a square castellated tower with thin buttresses, and cascades over rocks. On each side is a short stretch of wall over flatter arches and then two lower towers with battered bases. Despite its undoubted age, it is most unpicturesque, and the choice of dressed stone is inappropriate for this sort of feature. Behind the top lake is a matching ice-house, curiously located in the sun beside a rectangular tower with an elaborate window and a tiny pigeon hole. If this set of buildings are by Brown, they must be counted one of his rare failures. On the other hand, much more pleasing than the cascade is the rotunda-like entrance lodge, Bath Lodge, which was without doubt designed by James Wyatt in 1802.

BATH

Location At the junction of the A46, A36, A4 and A431.

Bath's appeal lies in its history, its architecture and its culture, where Roman grandeur and Georgian elegance fuse into exuberance. Blessed with natural hot springs of constant warm temperature (49 degrees C) and output (250,000 gallons a day) unique in Britain, Bath has attracted attention for thousands of years. Legend has it that King Bladud first discovered the curative powers of its waters, which healed his leprosy in c.500 BC, but it was the advanced engineering skills of the Romans which highlighted the allure of Bath's water. They constructed a series of baths with controlled water levels, a theatre, public buildings, and a temple to Sulis Minerva, Sulis the Celtic goddess of the springs and Minerva the Roman goddess of healing, renaming the city Aquae Sulis. It was aquae sulis - the waters of the sun - which gave Bath both its name and its fame though the Romans also mined Bath stone and transported it to other parts of Britain. Bath stone was used through the centuries, but was popularised immensely for town and country mansions by the rebuilding of Bath as a fashionable neo-Roman city in the eighteenth century.

In 1668, Samuel Pepys acclaimed Bath *'the prettiest city in the Kingdom'*, but the best was yet to come. Three self-made men were responsible for its transformation. The flamboyant and charismatic dictator Richard 'Beau' Nash came to the city in 1705 and for fifty years ruled the social scene under his honorary title of Master of Ceremonies, establishing the social airs and graces and publishing and enforcing a code of manners for visitors. Ralph Allen became the city's deputy postmaster in 1712, quickly rising to the position of chief postmaster. He made a personal fortune from reorganising the nation's postal services and bought the nearby Combe Down quarries, from which came much of the creamy limestone used to build Bath, whose vigorous expansion he promoted. John Wood the Elder arrived in the city in 1727, engaged by the energetic entrepreneur Allen, who also provided the financial backing for the ambitious young architect to make the city into one of Europe's architectural showpieces. His genius was to bring elegance and Palladian designs for many fine buildings but he died before his masterpiece, the Circus, adapted from the concept of an amphitheatre, consisting of three crescents arranged in a circle with an open centre, could be completed. It was left to his son, John the Younger, to carry out his father's plan. It proved to be an exceedingly smart address: politician, painter or explorer, the Circus was the place to be - Pitt, Livingstone, Clive of India and Gainsborough all lived here. John the Younger was responsible in 1767 for the magnificent Royal Crescent, the longest and conceivably the finest in Europe, curving round a cobbled street, with a vast lawn sloping down to Victoria Park. Though the Crescent was originally a speculative development aimed at the upwardly mobile of the day, John the Younger's Georgian buildings sweep through Bath in stunning symmetry.

Collectively, the three proved an irressistable formula for success. The rich and famous, and those aspiring, flocked to take the waters and enjoy the fashionable 'season', making it the centre of England's smart society. In this sense, the eighteenth century belonged to Bath.

One result was **Ralph Allen's Sham Castle** (Sheet 172 76696486). Allen was one of Bath's most elegant inhabitants, who augmented his fortune as a quarrymaster by an income of £12,000 per annum by revising the postal system A little of that huge fortune was spent on building his Sham Castle. Set high on the slope of Bathwick Hill, this perfect example of an eyecatcher looks proudly down on the glittering city. When it was built, alone on its hillside, it was sited so as to be seen from Allen's town-house in Old Lilliput Alley. Now, with new houses springing up all along the hill, it is difficult to pick out the Sham so at night the City Corporation, which was given the castle in 1921, proudly floodlights it.

It is not a big building, but it is remarkably well done. The design has been attributed to Sanderson Miller, and certainly he drew up plans for a sham castle for Allen in 1755, but this existing building is known to have been designed and built in 1762 by Richard Jones, Allen's clerk of works. The folly certainly achieves the visual effect its owner and designer strove for. However, despite its appearance from afar, the Sham Castle is in fact two-dimensional: two 'round' towers are really semi-circular; smaller square towers at either end of the facade offset the bulk of the central gatehouse; the whole edifice, with its blank windows and blank arrow-slits, looks blindly out over the city. No more than forty feet high and one hundred feet long, its frivolity and excellent state of preservation give it the air of a recently abandoned film set.

In 1835, on the slopes of Bathwick Hill, an imposing Victorian Greek Revival edifice was built by John Pinch the Younger for General Augustus Andrews, who had retired from the Indian army the year before. Andrews named his new house Vellore, referring to a small town north of Madras, a place probably associated with a high point in his military career. Extensive conservatories and hot houses (long since disappeared) were also built to provide the house with fruit and flowers. Andrews spent a large sum of money on landscaping the seven acres of gardens with specimen trees, and in 1836 an elaborate grotto was built, as a protection from the sun whilst the trees grew to size; indeed it is remarkably temperate even on the hottest summer's day. The dark, grey, perforated uncut Bath stone from Combe Down contrasts starkly with the smooth honey colour of that of the house, and encapsulates admirably the Gothick ideal. General and Mrs Andrews had no children and the house and contents were sold upon their deaths in 1860, since when the house, though used, gradually fell into disrepair. Though ample cover is now given by the giant mature cedars, this splendid grotto was renovated at considerable cost when Vellore became the central part of the Bath Spa Hotel in 1985, and today forms a focus to the quiet, sweeping entrance drive.

Almost as the grotto was being built, the fashion was over.

> *Everything in the shape of grottos, when they take the form of a cavern,*
> *is disagreeable, and injurious to health ... Grottos are very rarely to be*
> *coveted, either as picturesque objects or resting-places; a good summer-*
> *house being capable of quite as much rusticity, and far more comfort.*
> Edward Kemp [1858] *How To Lay Out A Garden.*

Beckford's Tower (Sheet 172   73696760) is a superb example of an eccentric building created by an eccentric personality.

William Beckford was born in 1760 and was only ten years old when his father died, leaving him a colossal fortune, including an annual income of £100,000 from sugar plantations in Jamaica.

As his mother did not wish to send him to school he was educated by tutors, which included music lessons from Wolfgang Amadeus Mozart, then nine years old, and instruction in architecture from Sir William Chambers. Later he travelled extensively in Europe. He became an accomplished linguist, and his best known novel, *Vathek,* was written in French. He spent vast sums of money on the family house, Fonthill Abbey in Wiltshire, where he commissioned the construction of an edifice many consider to be the definitive folly. This was an extraordinary building with a 276 foot tower which collapsed in 1825 shortly after Beckford moved to live at Bath when he retired from politics as a Member of Parliament, driven from his Gothick fantasy and huge romantic complex of park, associated buildings and grottos by relative poverty but also ostacized from society as a consequence of a scandalous *affaire* with the Honourable William (Kitty) Courtenay, later 9th Earl of Devon. He had gone to such considerable lengths to maintain the romantic tradition that the lawns of glades of the landscape were scythed at night by the light of torches, so that by day the natural illusion was maintained.

In Bath, he bought two houses in a fashionable street but with a large tract of land, perhaps anticipating the restrictions that town life might impose upon him after the spaciousness of Fonthill, and retirement to a sybaritic life. Living relatively modestly at 20, Lansdown Crescent, he devoted almost all his time to collecting books and works of art. H E Goodridge, a young architect friend of his, helped to make the houses more comfortable by uniting them via a bridge across the intervening lane. In the garden of this house still survives a Moorish summer-house, which was very probably designed by Beckford himself. Although not very wide, his new garden stretched for over a mile, and at the top of the hill he built a tower to house many of his treasures.

Unlike Fonthill, this one did not collapse and with its extensive gardens is the finest surviving example of Beckford's work. It was built to the neo-Classical designs of his friend Goodridge in 1825-26 for the views it commanded of the surrounding countryside from the belvedere room and the top of the lantern, rising to its height of 154 feet through a series of unpremeditated stages. It begins as a very plain, straightforward square tower for about two-thirds of its height, its severity offset by the house at its foot. Then comes an overhanging parapet, and above that three plain glazed windows on each side. To top it all, Beckford and Goodridge allowed full reign to their imaginations and built a replica of the Choragic Monument of Lysicrates in Athens, a favourite theme for many folly-builders. The columns here are cast-iron, and have a bluish tinge against the red-rust background of the rest of the lantern. At dusk, when the lights are on in the Tower, the effect is quite chilling.

The inside is as interesting as the exterior. At the foot of the Tower, and connected to it, is a building with several small rooms. One of them, the Sanctuary, described in *The Illustrated London News* of November 22, 1845, just before the contents were sold at auction, had

... an air of mystic gloom and magnificence,

while the others were all luxuriously furnished, a drawing room embellished with a collection of *objets d'art,* and a library. The garden was a

> *... shrubbery, kept with strict adherence to the wildness of nature: no trim walks, no nicely-edged borders are there, the paths being only such as are worn by the passenger's feet.*

The stair climbs with a shallow sweep to the first floor. Suddenly everything is black, with the stair and railing spiralling up in a stygian gloom. As the stairs ascend, the climb breaks for the views, first at the belvedere room from which the magnificent outlook is diminished by too much wood and stone; then another stage with tiny recessed windows through which almost nothing shows; lastly at the top of the lantern. Here one is not inconvenienced by a high wind - - Beckford prudently had hot air pumped up by a furnace - but his treatment of the views may trouble the modern explorer: each is tightly enclosed like the composition of a painting, while nowadays a great sweep is more *a la mode.*

Before he died in 1844, eccentric to the end, William Beckford expressed a wish to be buried in the Tower next to his dog, but his family were unable to get the land consecrated and his granite sarcophagus was taken to the cemetery at Lyncombe.
In 1848 the Bishop of Bath and Wells consecrated the land at Lansdown and Beckford's body was reburied close to the Tower; Goodridge is buried here, also.

The garden near the Tower is now a cemetery, but further away remains evidence of Beckford's style: the ride to the stables from the Embattled Gate with one of his three coats-of-arms, a lime avenue, part of the planting of an old quarry, and a grotto-tunnel seventy feet long.

At **Prior Park** (Sheet 172 76006350), Ralph Allen's success in creating a seamless *ensemble* of architecture and landscape was due as much to its natural as to its social setting. The pragmatic local business tycoon wanted a highly visible advertisement for the quality of the Bath stone from his adjacent quarries: a house *'which sees all Bath and which was built for all Bath to see'*, as Philip Thicknesse wrote in 1788. The dramatic site meant that Allen could save himself a good deal of time, trouble and money.

> *Instead of forcing nature to bend to art, he has pursued only what*
> *the natural situation has pointed out to him,*

commented *The Universal Magazine* in May, 1754.

This restored landscape garden, is a gem: twenty-eight secluded, remarkably little-known acres of perfection. It forms a most aesthetically pleasing walk through a Palladian landscape where Romantic beauty merges with Classical grandeur in a dramatic natural setting. The path winds its original course through a wilderness and hanging woods to the famous viewpoint beneath the front of the house, *'perhaps the finest view in the Kingdom'* according to the Revd. John Collinson in 1791. Every turn reveals a tantalising image.

As a focal figure in the country's most bustling, fashionable and frivolous spa, Allen had access to many of the leading political, literary, artistic and gardening figures of the day. Thomas Gainsborough and William Hoare were regular guests at the house, as were David Garrick and William Pitt the Elder. Both Samuel Richardson and Henry Fielding used Prior Park as models for fictional seats, in *The History of Sir Charles Grandison and Tom Jones* respectively. Crucially, in 1735, Allen befriended the poet and gardener Alexander Pope by offering to sponsor a new edition of his letters. Pope advocated *'the amiable Simplicity of unadorned Nature'*, employed, according to his 1713 essay in the *Guardian, 'by the Ancients in their Gardens.* Thereafter, he became a regular correspondent and visitor, sometimes for periods of months, until his death in 1744.

Miller's Sham Bridge

It was almost certainly Pope who, when Allen began planting the park seven years before he moved into his new house, suggested a wilderness area with a winding path on the west side of the valley. This was in stark contrast to the formal planting behind the house. Pope's wilderness accumulated a number of the architectural fancies of the day, including a grotto for Mrs. Allen, a vermiculated sham bridge by Sanderson Miller, a serpentine lake and a statue of Moses standing over a cascade into a round clearing known as the Cabinet.

After Pope's death, Allen's improvements continued at hectic pace as he attempted to keep up with the rapidly evolving artistic fashions and whims of the second generation of Whig aristocracy. The vogue for Gothic prompted an ornamental lodge and a temple (as well as the Sham Castle on one of Allen's other estates). Later, the taste for Chinese prompted the Rock Gate. Importantly, the park - which formerly terminated half-way down the valley in a round basin - was extended all the way down to the lakes at the valley floor; and which were enlarged using dams at three levels.

In 1755, a Palladian bridge was constructed over the nearest lake, giving the illusion of one continuous surface of water. A pen-and-water sketch of c.1758 by Thomas Robins shows a dramatic cascade running between the plantations which separated the upper and lower parts of the valley. Though it cannot be determined whether these were actually built or not, other contemporary visitors mention waterfalls: Defoe's 1748 *Tour Through the Whole Island of Great Britain* describes:

> *Below the House ... two terraces and two slopes ... and the affluence of water is so great that it is received in three places; and after many agreeable falls.*

Even developments as considerable as these did not last long. In the third, final phase of the garden, from 1760 until Allen's death in 1764, all such contrivances were swept away. The lawn was continued from the house down to the bridge and lakes in an uninterrupted sweep; the structural planting on either side was softened and naturalised. Improvements ceased, the garden was neglected, and many of the embellishments and follies were lost for ever.

Palladian Bridge

CORSHAM

Location South of the A4, nine miles north-east of Bath. Sheet 172 87437067

Corsham Court, a royal manor in the days of Saxon kings, is based on an Elizabethan house dating from 1582. In the mid-eighteenth century it was bought by Paul Methuen to house his collection of Italian and Flemish master paintings and statuary. It was remodelled later by John Nash but principally by Thomas Bellamy in 1844-49 for Lord Methuen, to receive a second collection of fashionable Italian masters, rare Italian primitives, and furniture.

The gardens were designed by Lancelot 'Capability' Brown, who also built the Gothic Bath House, laid out the avenues and provided for the specimen trees such as the Oriental Plane which now has a circumference of over 240 yards.

Bellamy had been a student under David Laing, who specialised in designing *'Picturesque'* buildings and *cottages ornees,* and this may explain the extraordinary edifice behind the stables, an enormous crinkle-crankle wall about sixty feet high and one hundred feet long. Evidently intended to convey an ecclesiastical air, it was built with stones from Chippenham Abbey, including some of the window tracery. Did it have any purpose? If it was meant to disguise the stables, then it fails quite gloriously: so blatant an object in this setting cries out to be investigated by the explorer. However, it is massively, solidly and carefully built, with Gothick chimneys perched on top looking as apparent after-thoughts, and is large enough to conceal small rooms in its base: did these prove useful as hen-houses? Details of the Gothick window tracery are far more prominent on the north side of the wall than the south, which may indicate that it was meant to be seen from the house.

It is by no means certain that Thomas Bellamy was the designer of this magnificent folly, but if not then who was?

THE AUTHORS

Eccentricity in all its forms, whether expressed in behaviour or manifest in buildings and gardens, has an appeal for us all. It has been of life-long interest to both authors and here they have concentrated their extensive researches onto an area where they have lived and worked for a combined total of over four decades. To this they have brought their fascination for our world of symbolism, given further impetus in the writing of this book. As in previous collaborative books, Margaret has contributed all the photographs and in this volume documents many examples of follies and fanciful buildings never before published.

Bliss and Sons Mill, Chipping Norton

INDEX